knitting basics 8

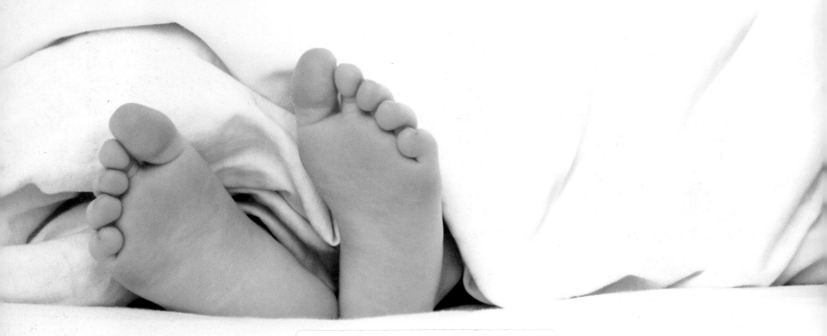

downtime 36

ballettop 38

cosysweater 44

tvblanket 50

ragdoll 52

alphabetcushions 58

zippedgilet 64

special time 70

time out 106

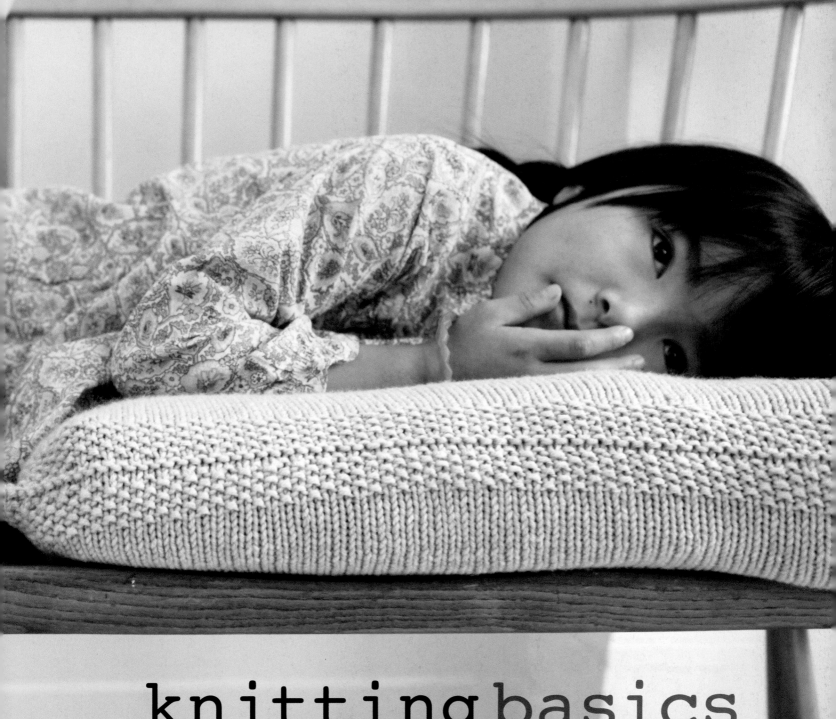

knittingbasics

types of yarns

When choosing a yarn for children's hand knits it is important that you work with a fibre that is soft but also practical. Children are often more used to the lightweight freedom of fleeces and they can be resistant to hand knits that they may consider scratchy and uncomfortable.

The yarns I have chosen for the designs in this book are either an extra fine merino or cashmere mixes. Although they create fabrics that are gentle against the skin, the other essential feature is that they are machine washable.

When knitting a garment always make the effort to buy the yarn stated in the pattern. All these designs have been created with a specific yarn in mind. A different yarn may not produce the same quality of fabric or have the same wash and wear properties. From an aesthetic point of view, the clarity of a subtle stitch pattern may be lost if a garment is knitted in an inferior yarn.

However, there may be occasions when a knitter needs to substitute a yarn – if there is an allergy to wool, for example – and so the following is a guideline to making the most informed choices.

Always buy a yarn that is the same weight as that given in the pattern: replace a double knitting with a double knitting, for example, and check that the tension of both yarns is the same.

Where you are substituting a different fibre, be aware of the design. A cable pattern knitted in cotton when worked in wool will pull in because of the greater elasticity of the yarn and so the fabric will become narrower; this will alter the proportions of the garment.

Check the metreage of the yarn. Yarns that weigh the same may have different lengths in the ball or hank, so you may need to buy more or less yarn.

Here are descriptions of my yarns and a guide to their weights and types:

Debbie Bliss baby cashmerino:
A lightweight yarn between a 4ply and a double knitting.
55% merino wool, 33% microfibre, 12% cashmere.
Approximately 125m/50g ball.
Debbie Bliss cashmerino aran:
55% merino wool, 33% microfibre, 12% cashmere.
Approximately 90m/50g ball.
Debbie Bliss cashmerino double knitting:
55% merino wool, 33% microfibre, 12% cashmere.
Approximately 110m/50g ball.
Debbie Bliss rialto double knitting:
100% merino wool extra fine superwash.
Approximately 105m/50g ball.

Debbie Bliss rialto aran:
100% merino wool extra fine superwash.
Approximately 80m/50g ball.

buying yarn

The ball band on the yarn will carry all the essential information you need as to tension, needle size, weight and yardage. Importantly it will also have the dye lot. Yarns are dyed in batches or lots, which can vary considerably. As your retailer may not have the same dye lot later on, buy all your yarn for a project at the same time. If you know that sometimes you use more yarn than that quoted in the pattern buy extra. If it is not possible to buy all the yarn you need with the same dye lot use the different ones where it will not show as much, on a neck or border, as a change of dye lot across a main piece will most likely show.

It is also a good idea at the time of buying the yarn that you check the pattern and make sure that you already have the needles you will require. If not buy them now, as it will save a lot of frustration when you get home.

garment care

Taking care of your hand knits is important because you want them to look good for as long as possible. Correct washing is particularly important for children's garments as they need to be washed often.

Check the ball band on the yarn for washing instructions to see whether the yarn is hand or machine washable, and if it is the latter, at what temperature it should be washed.

Most hand knits should be dried flat on an absorbent cloth, such as a towel, to soak up any moisture. Lying them flat in this way gives you an opportunity to pat the garment back into shape if it has become pulled around in the washing machine. Even if you are in a hurry, do not be tempted to dry your knits near a direct heat source, such as a radiator.

As children's garments are small, you may prefer to hand wash them. Use a washing agent that is specifically designed for knitwear as this will be kinder to the fabric. Use warm rather than hot water and handle the garment gently without rubbing or wringing. Let the water out of the basin and then gently squeeze out the excess water. Do not lift out a water-logged knit as the weight of the water will pull it out of shape. You may need to remove more moisture by rolling in a towel. Dry flat as before.

techniques

cast on

Your first step when beginning to knit is to work a foundation row called a cast-on. Without this row you cannot begin to knit.

There are several methods of casting on, each can be suited to a particular purpose or is chosen because the knitter feels comfortable with that particular technique. The two examples shown here are the ones I have found to be the most popular, the thumb and the cable methods.

In order to work a cast-on edge, you must first make a slip-knot.

slip-knot

1 Wind the yarn around the fingers on your left hand to make a circle of yarn as shown above. With the knitting needle, pull a loop of the yarn attached to the ball through the yarn circle on your fingers.

2 Pull both ends of the yarn to tighten the slip-knot on the knitting needle. You are now ready to begin, using either of the following cast-on techniques.

cast on

thumb cast-on

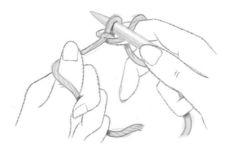

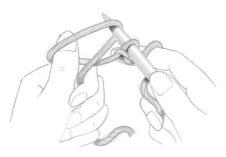

1 Make a slip-knot as shown on page 13, leaving a long tail. With the slip-knot on the needle in your right hand and the yarn that comes from the ball over your index finger, wrap the tail end of the yarn over your left thumb from front to back, holding the yarn in your palm with your fingers.

2 Insert the knitting needle upwards through the yarn loop on your left thumb.

The thumb cast-on is a one needle method that produces a flexible edge, which makes it particularly useful when using non-elastic yarns such as cotton. The 'give' in it also makes it a good one to use where the edge will turn back, as on the cuffs of the scarf coat (see page 136).

Unlike two needle methods you are working toward the yarn end, which means you have to predict the length you need to cast on the required amount of stitches. Otherwise you may find you do not have enough yarn to complete the last few stitches and have to start all over again. If unsure always allow for more yarn than you think you need as you can use what is left over for sewing up.

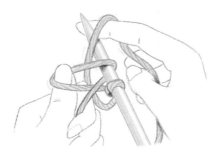

3 With the right index finger, wrap the yarn from the ball up and over the point of the knitting needle.

4 Draw the yarn through the loop on your thumb to form a new stitch on the knitting needle. Then, let the yarn loop slip off your left thumb and pull the loose end to tighten up the stitch. Repeat these steps until the required number of stitches have been cast on.

cable cast-on

1 Make a slip-knot as shown on page 13. Hold the knitting needle with the slip-knot in your left hand and insert the right-hand needle from left to right and from front to back through the slip-knot. Wrap the yarn from the ball up and over the point of the right-hand needle as shown.

2 With the right-hand needle, draw a loop through the slip-knot to make a new stitch. Do not drop the stitch from the left-hand needle, but instead slip the new stitch onto the left-hand needle as shown.

The cable cast-on method uses two needles and is particularly good for ribbed edges, as it provides a sturdy, but still elastic, edge. As you need to insert the needle between the stitches and pull the yarn through to create another stitch make sure that you do not make the new stitch too tight. The cable method is one of the most widely used cast-ons.

3 Next, insert the right-hand needle between the two stitches on the left-hand needle and wrap the yarn around the point of the right-hand needle.

4 Pull the yarn through to make a new stitch, and then place the new stitch on the left-hand needle, as before. Repeat the last two steps until the required number of stitches have been cast on.

knit
& purl

The knit and purl stitches form the basis of almost all knitted fabrics. The knit stitch is the easiest to learn and is the first stitch you will create. When worked continuously it forms a reversible fabric called garter stitch. You can recognise garter stitch by the horizontal ridges formed at the top of the knitted loops.

After the knit stitch you will move onto the purl stitch. If you work the purl stitch continuously it forms the same fabric as garter stitch. However if you alternate the purl rows with knit rows it creates stocking stitch, which is the most widely used knitted fabric.

knit

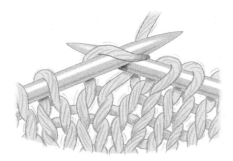 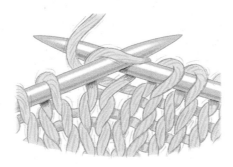 

1 With the cast-on stitches on the needle in your left hand, insert the right-hand needle from left to right and from front to back through the first cast-on stitch.

2 Take the yarn from the ball on your index finger (the working yarn) around the point of the right-hand needle.

3 Draw the right-hand needle and yarn through the stitch, thus forming a new stitch on the right-hand needle, and at the same time slip the original stitch off the left-hand needle. Repeat these steps until all the stitches from the left-hand needle have been worked. One knit row has now been completed.

purl

1 With the yarn to the front of the work, insert the right-hand needle from the right to the left into the front of the first stitch on the left-hand needle.

2 Then take the yarn from the ball on your index finger (the working yarn) around the point of the right-hand needle.

3 Draw the right-hand needle and the yarn through the stitch, thus forming a new stitch on the right-hand needle, and at the same time slip the original stitch off the left-hand needle. Repeat these steps until all the stitches have been worked. One purl row has now been completed.

increase

Increases are used to add to the width of the knitted fabric by creating more stitches. They are worked, for example, when shaping sleeves up the length of the arm or when additional stitches are needed after a ribbed welt. Some increases are invisible, while others are worked away from the edge of the work and are meant to be seen in order to give decorative detail. Most knitting patterns will tell you which type of increase to make.

increase one ('kfb')

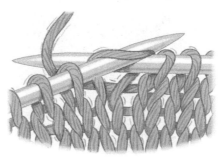

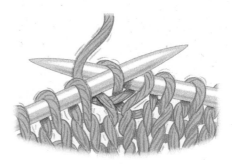

1 Insert the right-hand needle into the front of the next stitch, then knit the stitch but leave it on the left-hand needle.

2 Insert the right-hand needle into the back of the same stitch and knit it. Then slip the original stitch off the needle. Now you have made an extra stitch on the right-hand needle.

make one ('m1')

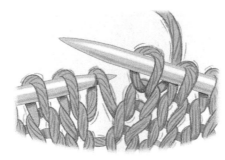

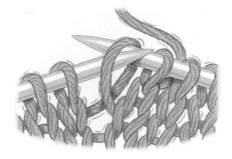

1 Insert the left-hand needle from front to back under the horizontal strand between the stitch just worked on the right-hand needle and the first stitch on the left-hand needle.

2 Knit into the back of the loop to twist it, and to prevent a hole. Drop the strand from the left-hand needle. This forms a new stitch on the right-hand needle.

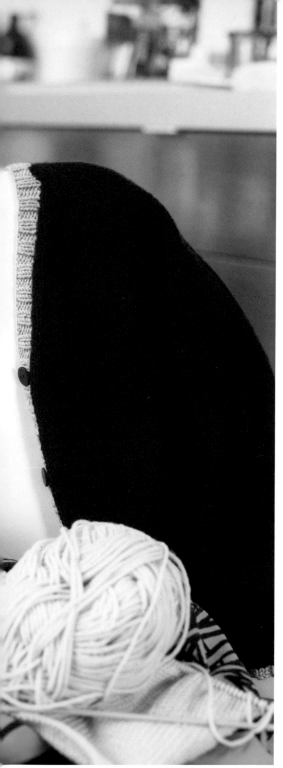

yarn over ('yf', 'yo', 'yrn')

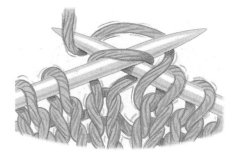

yarn over between knit stitches
Bring the yarn forward between
the two needles, from the back to
the front of the work. Taking the
yarn over the right-hand needle
to do so, knit the next stitch.

yarn over between purl stitches
Bring the yarn over the right-hand
needle to the back, then between the
two needles to the front. Then purl
the next stitch.

yarn over between a purl and a knit
Take the yarn from the front over
the right-hand needle to the back.
Then knit the next stitch.

yarn over between a knit and a purl
Bring the yarn forward between the
two needles from the back to the front
of the work, and take it over the top
of the right-hand needle to the back
again and then forward between the
needles. Then purl the next stitch.

cast off

knit cast off

1 Knit two stitches. Insert the left-hand needle into the first stitch knitted on the right-hand needle and lift this stitch over the second stitch and off the right-hand needle.

2 One stitch is now on the right-hand needle. Knit the next stitch. Repeat the first step until all the stitches have been cast off. Pull the yarn through the last stitch to fasten off.

purl cast off

Cast off is used to finish off your knitted piece so that the stitches don't unravel. It is also used to decrease more than one stitch at a time, such as when shaping armholes, neckbands, and buttonholes. It is important that a cast off is firm but elastic, particularly when casting off around a neckband, to ensure that it can be pulled easily over the head. Unless told otherwise, cast off in the pattern used in the piece.

1 Purl two stitches. Insert the left-hand needle into the front of the first stitch worked on the right-hand needle and lift this stitch over the second stitch and off the right-hand needle.

2 One stitch is now on the right-hand needle. Purl the next stitch. Repeat the first step until all the stitches have been cast off. Pull the yarn through the last stitch to fasten off.

decrease

Decreases are used to make the fabric narrower by getting rid of stitches on the needle. They are worked to make an opening for a neckline or shaping a sleeve head. As with increases they can be used to create decorative detail, often around a neck edge. Increases and decreases are used together to create lace patterns.

knit 2 together

knit 2 together ('k2tog' or 'dec one')
On a knit row, insert the right-hand needle from left to right through the next two stitches on the left-hand needle and knit them together. One stitch has been decreased.

purl 2 together

purl 2 together ('p2tog' or 'dec one')
On a purl row, insert the right-hand needle from right to left through the next two stitches on the left-hand needle. Then purl them together. One stitch has been decreased.

slip stitch over

slip 1, knit 1, pass slipped stitch over ('psso')
1 Insert the right-hand needle into the next stitch on the left-hand needle and slip it onto the right-hand needle without knitting it. Knit the next stitch. Then insert the left-hand needle into the slipped stitch as shown.

2 With the left-hand needle, lift the slipped stitch over the knitted stitch as shown and off the right-hand needle.

reading patterns

To those unfamiliar with knitting patterns they can appear to be written in a strange, alien language! However as you become used to the terminology you will see that they have a logic and consistency that you will soon become familiar with.

Do not be too concerned if you read through a pattern first and are confused by parts of it as some instructions make more sense when your stitches are on the needle and you are at that point in the piece. However, it is sometimes a good idea to check with your retailer whether your skill levels are up to a particular design as this can prevent frustration later on.

Figures for larger sizes are given in round ( ) brackets. Where only one figure appears it means that those numbers apply to all sizes. Figures in square brackets [ ] are to be worked the number of times stated after the brackets. Where 0 appears, no stitches or rows are worked for this size.

When following the pattern it is important you consistently use the right stitches or rows for your size, and you don't switch inside the brackets. Avoid this by marking off your size throughout with a highlighting pen, but photocopy the pattern first so that you don't spoil your book.

Before starting your project check the size and the actual measurements that are quoted for that size, you may want to make a smaller or larger garment depending on the proportions of the wearer it is intended for.

The quantities of yarn quoted in the instructions are based on the yarn used by the knitter of the original garment and therefore all amounts should be considered approximate. For example, if that knitter has used almost all of the last ball, it may be that another knitter with a slightly different tension has to break into another ball to complete the garment. A slight variation in tension can therefore make the difference between using fewer or more balls than that stated in the pattern.

tension

Every knitting pattern will state a tension or gauge – the number of stitches and rows to 10cm that should be obtained with the quoted yarn, needle size and stitch pattern. It is vital to check your tension before starting your project. A slight variation can alter the proportions of the finished garment and the look of the fabric. A too loose tension will produce an uneven and unstable fabric that can drop or lose its shape after washing, whilst a too tight tension can make a hard, inelastic fabric.

Making a tension square

Use the same needles, yarn and stitch pattern quoted in the tension note in the pattern. Knit a sample at last 13cm square to get the most accurate result. Smooth out the finished sample on a flat surface making sure you are not stretching it out. To check the stitch tension place a tape measure or ruler horizontally on the sample and mark 10cm with pins. Count the number of stitches between the pins. To check the row tension mark 10cm with pins vertically as before and count the number of rows. If the number of stitches and rows is greater than that quoted in the pattern, your tension is tighter and you should try changing to a larger needle and trying another tension square. If there are fewer stitches and rows, your tension is looser and you should try again on a smaller needle. The stitch tension is the most important to get right as the number of stitches in a pattern are set but the length is often calculated in measurement rather than rows and you may be able to work more or fewer rows.

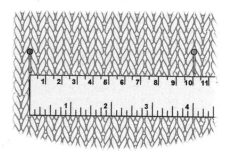

abbreviations

In a pattern book general abbreviations
will usually be given at the front before
the patterns begin, whilst those more
specific to a particular design will
be given at the start of the individual
pattern. The following are the ones
used throughout this book.

standard abbreviations

alt = alternate
beg = begin(ning)
cont = continue
dec = decrease (ing)
foll = following
inc = increase (ing)
k = knit
kfb = knit into front and back of next st
m1 = make one stitch by picking up
the loop lying between the stitch
just worked and the next stitch and
working into the back of it
patt = pattern
p = purl
psso = pass slipped stitch over
rem = remain (ing)
rep = repeat (ing)
skpo = slip 1, knit 1, pass slipped
stitch over
sl = slip
st(s) = stitch(es)
st st = stocking stitch
tbl = through back of loop
tog = together
yf = yarn forward
yon = yarn over needle
yrn = yarn round needle

cables

back cross 6 stitch cable ('C6B')

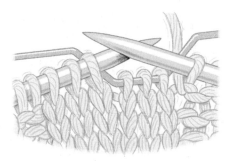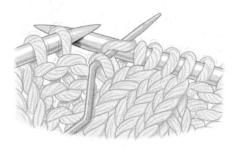

1 Slip the first three cable stitches purlwise off the left-hand needle and onto the cable needle. Leave the cable needle at the back of the work, then knit the next three stitches on the left-hand needle, keeping the yarn tight to prevent a gap from forming in the knitting.

2 Knit the three stitches directly from the cable needle, or if preferred, slip the three stitches from the cable needle back onto the left-hand needle and then knit them. This completes the cable cross.

front cross 6 stitch cable ('C6F')

Cables are formed by the simple technique of crossing one set of stitches over another. Stitches are held on a cable needle (a short double-pointed needle) at the back or front of the work while the same amount of stitches is worked from the left-hand needle. Simple cables form a vertical twisted rope of stocking stitch on a background of reverse stocking stitch and tend to be worked over four or six stitches.

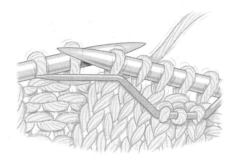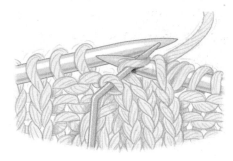

1 Slip the first three cable stitches purlwise off the left-hand needle and onto the cable needle. Leave the cable needle at the front of the work, then knit the next three stitches on the left-hand needle, keeping the yarn tight to prevent a gap from forming in the knitting.

2 Knit the three stitches directly from the cable needle, or if preferred, slip the three stitches from the cable needle back onto the left-hand needle and then knit them. This completes the cable cross.

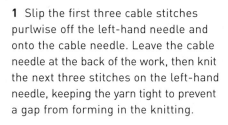

intarsia

Intarsia is used when you are working with larger areas of usually isolated colour, such as when knitting motifs. If the yarn not in use was stranded or woven behind, it could show through to the front or pull in the colour work. In intarsia you use a separate strand or small ball of yarn for each colour area and then twist them together where they meet to prevent a gap forming.

vertical

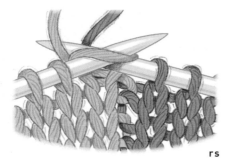

rs

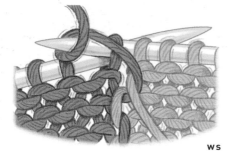

ws

changing colours on a vertical line
If the two colour areas are forming a vertical line, to change colours on a knit row drop the colour you were using. Pick up the new colour and wrap it around the dropped colour as shown, then continue with the new colour. Twist the yarns together on knit and purl rows in this same way at vertical-line colour changes.

right diagonal

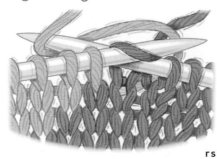

rs

ws

changing colours on a right diagonal
If the two colour areas are forming a right diagonal line, on a knit row drop the colour you were using. Pick up the new colour and wrap it around the dropped colour as shown, then continue with the new colour. Twist the yarns together on knit rows only at right-diagonal colour changes.

left diagonal

rs

ws

changing colours on a left diagonal
If the two colour areas are forming a left diagonal line, on a purl row drop the colour you were using. Pick up the new colour and wrap it around the colour just dropped as shown, then continue with the new colour. Twist the yarns together on purl rows only at left-diagonal colour changes.

reading charts

Most colour patterns are worked from a chart rather than set out in the text. Each square represents a stitch and row and the symbol or colour within it will tell you which colour to use. There will be a key listing the symbols used and the colours they represent.

2nd size left front

2nd size right front

8 st patt rep

all sizes back, 1st and 3rd sizes left and right front

Unless stated otherwise, the first row of the chart is worked from right to left and represents the first right side row of your knitting. The second chart row represents the second and wrong side row and is read and worked from left to right.

If the colour pattern is a repeated design, as in Fairisle, the chart will tell you how many stitches are in each repeat. You will repeat these stitches as many times as is required. At each side of the repeat there may be edge stitches, these are only worked at the beginning and end of the rows and they indicate where you need to start and end for the piece you are knitting. Most colour patterns are worked in stocking stitch.

M pale pink   A mid green   B pale green

C ecru   D mid pink   E lemon   F chocolate

stranding

Stranding is used when colour is worked over a small amount of stitches where using two colours in a row. The colour you are not using is left hanging on the wrong side of the work and then picked up when it is needed again. This creates strands at the back of the work called floats. Care must be taken so that they are not pulled too tightly as this will pucker the fabric. By picking up the yarns over and under one another you will prevent them tangling.

stranding on a knit row

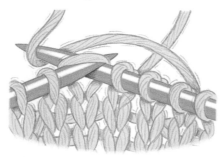 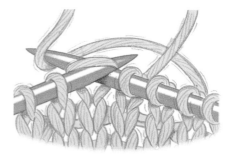

1 On a right-side (knit) row, to change colours drop the colour you were using. Pick up the new colour, take it over the top of the dropped colour and start knitting with it.

2 To change back to the old colour, drop the colour you were knitting with. Pick up the old colour, take it under the dropped colour and knit to the next colour change, and so on.

stranding on a purl row

1 On a wrong-side (purl) row, to change colours drop the colour you were using. Pick up the new colour, take it over the top of the dropped colour and start purling with it.

2 To change back to the old colour, drop the colour you were knitting with. Pick up the old colour, take it under the dropped colour and purl to the next colour change, and so on.

&weaving in

weaving in on a knit row

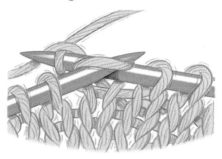 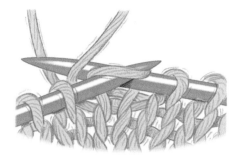

1 To weave in yarn on a knit stitch, insert the right-hand needle into the next stitch and lay the yarn to be woven in over the right-hand needle. Knit the stitch with the working yarn, taking it under the yarn not in use and making sure you do not catch this strand into the knitted stitch.

2 Knit the next stitch with the working yarn, taking it over the yarn being woven in. Continue like this, weaving the loose colour over and under the working yarn alternately with each stitch until you need to use it again.

weaving in on a purl row

When there are more than four stitches between a colour change, the floats are too long and this makes the fabric inflexible. The long strands can also catch when wearing the garment, particularly on the inside of a sleeve. By weaving in, the yarn not in use is caught up before the next colour change, thus shortening the float. Sometimes, depending on the colour pattern, a combination of both stranding and weaving can be used.

1 To weave in yarn on a purl stitch, insert the right-hand needle into the next stitch and lay the yarn to be woven in over the right-hand needle. Purl the stitch with the working yarn, taking it under the yarn not in use and making sure you do not catch this strand into the purled stitch.

2 Purl the next stitch with the working yarn, taking it over the yarn being woven in. Continue like this, weaving the loose colour over and under the working yarn alternately with each stitch until you need to use it again.

seaming

When you have completed the pieces of your knitting you reach one of the most important stages. The way you sew up or finish your project determines how good your finished garment will look. There are different types of seaming techniques but the best by far is mattress or ladder stitch, which creates an invisible seam. It can be used on stocking stitch, rib, garter and moss stitch.

The seam that I use for almost all sewing up is mattress stitch, which produces a wonderful invisible seam. It works well on any yarn, and makes a completely straight seam, as the same amount is taken up on each side – this also means that the knitted pieces should not need to be pinned together first. It is always worked on the right side of the fabric and is particularly useful for sewing up stripes and Fairisle.

I use other types of seams less frequently, but they do all have their uses. For instance, backstitch can sometimes be useful for sewing in a sleeve head, to neatly ease in the fullness.

It is also good for catching in loose strands of yarn on colourwork seams, where there can be a lot of short ends along the selvedge. Just remember when using backstitch to sew up your knitting that it is important to ensure that you work in a completely straight line.

The seam for joining two cast-off edges is handy for shoulder seams, while the seam for joining a cast-off edge with a side edge (selvedge) is usually used when sewing a sleeve onto the body on a dropped shoulder style.

It is best to leave a long tail at the casting-on stage to sew up your knitting with, so that the sewing up yarn is already secured in place. If this

is not possible, when first securing the thread for the seam, you should leave a length that can be darned in afterwards. All seams on knitting should be sewn with a large blunt-tipped yarn or tapestry needle to avoid splitting the yarn.

Before sewing up side seams, join the shoulder seams and attach the sleeves, unless they are set in sleeves. If there are any embellishments, such as applied pockets or embroidery, this is the time to put them on, when you can lay the garment out flat.

seams

mattress stitch on stocking stitch and double rib
With the right sides of the knitting facing you, insert the needle under the horizontal bar between the first stitch and next stitch. Then insert the needle under the same bar on the other piece. Continue to do this, drawing up the thread to form the seam.

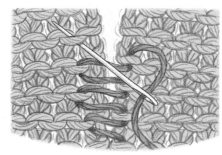

mattress stitch on garter stitch
With the right sides of the knitting facing you, insert the needle through the bottom of the 'knot' on the edge and then through the top of the corresponding 'knot' on the opposite edge. Continue to do this from edge to edge, drawing up the thread to form a flat seam.

mattress stitch on moss stitch
With the right sides of the knitting facing you, insert the needle under the horizontal bar between the first and second stitches on one side and through the top of the 'knot' on the edge of the opposite side.

joining two cast-off edges (grafting)
1 With the cast-off edges butted together, bring the needle out in the centre of the first stitch just below the cast-off edge on one piece. Insert the needle through the centre of the first stitch on the other piece and out through the centre of the next stitch.

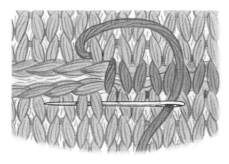

2 Next, insert the needle through the centre of the first stitch on the first piece again and out through the centre of the stitch next to it. Continue in this way until the seam is completed.

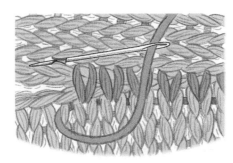

joining cast-off and selvedge edges
Bring the needle back to front through the centre of the first stitch on the cast-off edge. Then insert it under one or two horizontal strands between the first and second stitches on the selvedge and back through the centre of the same cast-off stitch. Continue in this way until the seam is completed.

pickingupstitches

When you are adding a border to your garment, such as front bands or a neckband, you usually pick up stitches around the edge. A border can be sewn on afterwards but this method is far neater. If you are picking up stitches along a long edge, a front band of a jacket for example, a long circular needle can be used so that you can fit all the stitches on. The pattern will usually tell you how many stitches to pick up.

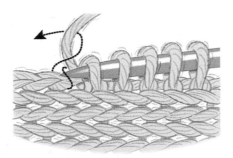

picking up stitches along a selvedge
With the right side of the knitting facing, insert the knitting needle from front to back between the first and second stitches of the first row. Wrap the yarn around the needle and pull a loop through to a form a new stitch on the needle. Continue in this way along the edge of the knitting.

picking up stitches along a neck edge
On a neck edge, work along the straight edges as for a selvedge. But along the curved edges, insert the needle through the centre of the stitch below the shaping (to avoid large gaps) and pull a loop of yarn through to form a new stitch on the needle.

downtime

measurements

To fit ages 2–3 (3–4: 4–5) years

actual measurements

Chest 61 (66: 71)cm

Length to shoulder 29 (32: 35)cm

Sleeve length 16 (19: 23)cm

materials

4 (5: 6) x 50g balls Debbie Bliss Baby Cashmerino in ecru

Pair each 2³/₄mm and 3¹/₄mm knitting needles

tension

25 sts and 34 rows to 10cm square over st st using 3¹/₄mm needles.

abbreviations

See page 23.

ballet top

back

With 2³/₄mm needles, cast on 69 (73: 77) sts.

K 5 rows.

Change to 3¹/₄mm needles.

Beg with a k row, work 6 rows in st st.

Inc row K3, m1, k to last 3 sts, m1, k3.

Work 7 rows in st st.

Rep the last 8 rows 3 (4: 5) times more then inc row again. 79 (85: 91) sts.

Cont straight until back measures 18 (20: 22)cm from cast-on edge, ending with a p row.

Shape armholes

Cast off 5 sts at beg of next 2 rows and 4 sts at beg of foll 2 rows. 61 (67: 73) sts.

Next row K3, skpo, k to last 5 sts, k2tog, k3.

Next row P to end.

Rep the last 2 rows 2 (3: 4) times more. 55 (59: 63) sts.

Cont straight until back measures 29 (32: 35)cm from cast-on edge, ending with a p row.

Shape shoulders

Cast off 8 (8: 9) sts at beg of next 2 rows and 7 (8: 8) sts at beg of foll 2 rows.

Cast off rem 25 (27: 29) sts.

left front

With 2³/₄mm needles, cast on 59 (63: 67) sts.

K 5 rows.

Change to 3¹/₄mm needles.

Next row K to end.

Next row K3, p to end.

Rep the last 2 rows twice more.

Inc row (right side) K3, m1, k to last 3 sts, m1, k3.

Work 7 rows as set.

Rep the last 8 rows 1 (2: 3) times more then the inc row once again. 65 (71: 77) sts.

Shape neck

Next row (wrong side) Cast off 9 sts, p to end. 56 (62: 68) sts.

Next row K to last 3 sts, k2tog, k1.

Next row P to end.

Rep the last 2 rows twice more. 53 (59: 65) sts.

Next row K3, m1, k to last 3 sts, k2tog, k1.

Next row P to end.

Cont in st st and dec 1 st at neck edge on every right side row, **at the same time** work one more side edge inc on the foll 7th row then keep side edge straight and work until front measures 18 (20: 22)cm from cast-on edge, ending with a p row.

Shape armhole

Next row (right side) Cast off 5 sts, k to last 3 sts, k2tog, k1.

Next row P to end.

Next row Cast off 4 sts, k to last 3 sts, k2tog, k1.

Next row P to end.

Next row K3, skpo, k to last 3 sts, k2tog, k1.

Next row P to end.

Rep the last 2 rows 2 (3: 4) times more.

Keeping armhole edge straight, cont to dec 1 st at neck edge on every right side row until 15 (16: 17) sts remain.

Work straight until front measures same as Back to shoulder, ending at armhole edge.

Shape shoulder

Cast off 8 (8: 9) sts at beg of next row.

Work 1 row.

Cast off rem 7 (8: 8) sts.

right front

With 2³/₄mm needles, cast on 59 (63: 67) sts.

K 5 rows.

Change to 3¹/₄mm needles.

Next row K to end.

Next row P to last 3 sts, k3.

Rep the last 2 rows twice more.

Inc row K3, m1, k to last 3 sts, m1, k3.

Work 7 rows as set.

Rep the last 8 rows 1 (2: 3) times more then the inc row once again. 65 (71: 77) sts.

Work 1 row.
Shape neck
Next row (right side) Cast off 9 sts, k to end. 56 (62: 68) sts.
Next row P to end.
Next row K1, skpo, k to end.
Next row P to end.
Rep the last 2 rows once more. 54 (60: 66) sts.
Next row K1, skpo, k to last 3 sts, m1, k3.
Next row P to end.
Cont in st st and dec 1 st at neck edge on every right side row, **at the same time** work one more side edge inc on the foll 7th row then keep side edge straight and work until front measures 18 (20: 22)cm from cast-on edge, ending with a k row.
Shape armhole
Next row (wrong side) Cast off 5 sts, p to end.
Next row K1, skpo, k to end.
Next row Cast off 4 sts, p to end.
Next row K1, skpo, k to last 5 sts, k2tog, k3.
Next row P to end.
Rep the last 2 rows 2 (3: 4) times more.
Keeping armhole edge straight, cont to dec 1 st at neck edge on every right side row until 15 (16: 17) sts remain.
Work straight until front measures same as Back to shoulder, ending at armhole edge.
Shape shoulder
Cast off 8 (8: 9) sts at beg of next row.
Work 1 row.
Cast off rem 7 (8: 8) sts.

sleeves

With 2³/₄mm needles, cast on 46 (50: 54) sts.
K 5 rows.
Change to 3¹/₄mm needles.
Beg with a k row, work 4 rows in st st.
Inc row K3, m1, k to last 3 sts, m1, k3.
Work 5 rows.
Rep the last 6 rows 6 (7: 8) times more and the inc row again. 62 (68: 74) sts.
Cont straight until sleeve measures 16 (19: 23)cm from cast-on edge, ending with a p row.
Shape sleeve top
Cast off 5 sts at beg of next 2 rows and 4 sts on foll 2 rows. 44 (50: 56) sts.
Next row K3, skpo, k to last 5 sts, k2tog, k3.
Next row P to end.
Next row K to end.
Next row P to end.
Rep the last 4 rows 0 (1: 1) time more and then the first 2 rows 1 (0: 1) time. 40 (46: 50) sts.
Cast off.

front edging

Join shoulder seams.
With right side facing and $2^3/_4$mm needles, pick up and k9 sts from cast-off edge of right front, pick up and k57 (63: 69) sts up right front neck, 25 (27: 29) sts from back neck, 57 (63: 69) sts down left front neck, then 9 sts from left front cast-off edge. 157 (171: 185) sts.
K 3 rows.
Cast off row Cast off 3 sts, * slip st back onto left-hand needle, cast on 2 sts, cast off 6 sts; rep from * to end.

ties (make 2)

With $2^3/_4$mm needles, cast on 125 (135: 145) sts.
K 3 rows.
Cast off.

to make up

Sew sleeves into armholes easing to fit. Join side and sleeve seams, leaving small opening in right seam level with beginning of neck shaping. Sew ties to ends of front edging.

cosy sweater

measurements
To fit ages 2–3 (3–4: 4–5) years
actual measurements
Chest 70 (75: 80)cm
Length to shoulder 38 (42: 46)cm
Sleeve length 22 (25: 28)cm

materials
6 (7: 8) x 50g balls Debbie Bliss Rialto Aran in lime (M)
1 (1: 1) x 50g ball Debbie Bliss Rialto Aran in stone (C)
Pair each 4^1/$_2$mm and 5mm knitting needles
Set of 4^1/$_2$mm double-pointed needles
2 buttons

tension
18 sts and 24 rows to 10cm square over st st using 5mm needles.

abbreviations
See page 23.

back

With 4¹/₂mm needles and C, cast on 66 (70: 74) sts.
K 1 row.
Change to M.
1st rib row (right side) K to end.
2nd rib row P2, [k2, p2] to end.
3rd rib row K2, [p2, k2] to end.
4th rib row P2, [k2, p2] to end.
K 4 rows.
Change to 5mm needles.
Beg with a k row, work in st st until back measures 22 (23: 24)cm from cast-on edge, ending with
a p row.
Shape raglan armholes
Cast off 3 sts at beg of next 2 rows. 60 (64: 68) sts.
1st row K3, skpo, k to last 5 sts, k2tog, k3.
2nd row P3, p2tog, p to last 5 sts, p2tog tbl, p3.
Rep the last 2 rows 5 times more. 36 (40: 44) sts.
Next row K3, skpo, k to last 5 sts, k2tog, k3.
Next row P to end. **
Rep the last 2 rows until 22 (24: 26) sts rem, ending with a p row.
Leave these sts on a holder.

front

Work as given for Back to **.
Rep the last 2 rows 0 (1: 2) times more. 34 (36: 38) sts.
Next row (right side) Cast off 2 sts, skpo, k to last 5 sts, k2tog, k3.
Next row P to end.
Next row K1, skpo, k to last 5 sts, k2tog, k3.
Rep the last 2 rows until 20 (22: 24) sts rem, ending with a p row.
Leave these sts on a holder.

right sleeve

With 4¹/₂mm needles and C, cast on 30 (34: 38) sts.
K 1 row.
Change to M.
1st rib row (right side) K to end.
2nd rib row P2, [k2, p2] to end.
3rd rib row K2, [p2, k2] to end.
4th rib row P2, [k2, p2] to end.
K 4 rows.
Change to 5mm needles.
Beg with a k row, work 4 (6: 8) rows in st st.
Inc row K3, m1, k to last 3 sts, m1, k3.
Beg with a p row, work 5 rows in st st.
Rep the last 6 rows 5 (6: 7) times more and the inc row again. 44 (50: 56) sts.
Cont straight until sleeve measures 22 (25: 28)cm from cast-on edge, ending with a p row.

Shape raglan top
Cast off 3 sts at beg of next 2 rows. *** 38 (44: 50) sts.
1st row K3, skpo, k to last 5 sts, k2tog, k3.
2nd row P to end.
Rep the last 2 rows until 12 (16: 20) sts rem, ending with a p row.
Leave these sts on a holder.

left sleeve

Work as given for Right Sleeve to ***.
1st row K3, skpo, k to last 5 sts, k2tog, k3.
2nd row P to end.
Rep the last 2 rows until 24 (28: 32) sts rem, ending with a p row.
Next row K3, skpo, k to last 5 sts, k2tog, k3.
Next row Cast off 2 sts, p to end.
Next row P to end.
Next row K3, skpo, k to last 3 sts, k2tog, k1.
Rep the last 2 rows until 10 (14: 18) sts rem, ending with a p row.
Leave these sts on a holder.

collar

With right side facing, 4¹/₂ mm needles and M, k19 (21: 23) sts from front holder, k last st of front tog with first st of right sleeve, k10 (14: 18), k last st of sleeve with first st of back, k9 (10: 11), k2tog, k9 (10: 11), k last st of back tog with first st of left sleeve, k9 (13: 17). 60 (72: 84) sts.
Next row K3, * p2, k2; rep from * to last 5 sts, p2, k3.
Next row P3, * k2, p2; rep from * to last 5 sts, k2, p3.
Rep the last 2 rows 7 times more and the 1st row again.
K 3 rows. Cast off.

button band

Join right front and both back raglan seams. Join left front raglan as far as cast-off sts.
With right side facing, 4¹/₂ mm double-pointed needles and M, pick up and k12 sts along left sleeve edge from start of collar to cast-off sts, break yarn, then with right side of collar facing, a second double-pointed needle and M, pick up and k18 sts along edge of collar from start of collar to cast-off edge. 30 sts.
1st row (wrong side of collar, right side of sweater) P2, [k2, p2] to end.
2nd row K2, [p2, k2] to end.
3rd row As 1st row.
Change to C.
4th row P12, k18.
5th row K18, p12.
Cast off row Cast off 12 sts purlwise, then 18 sts knitwise.

buttonhole band

With right side facing, 4¹/₂ mm double-pointed needles and M, pick up and k12 sts along left front edge to start of collar, break off yarn. With right side facing, a second double-pointed needle and M, pick up and k18 sts along edge of collar from cast-off edge to start of collar, break yarn then slip the 12 sts onto this needle. 30 sts.
Return to the top of collar and main ball of yarn.

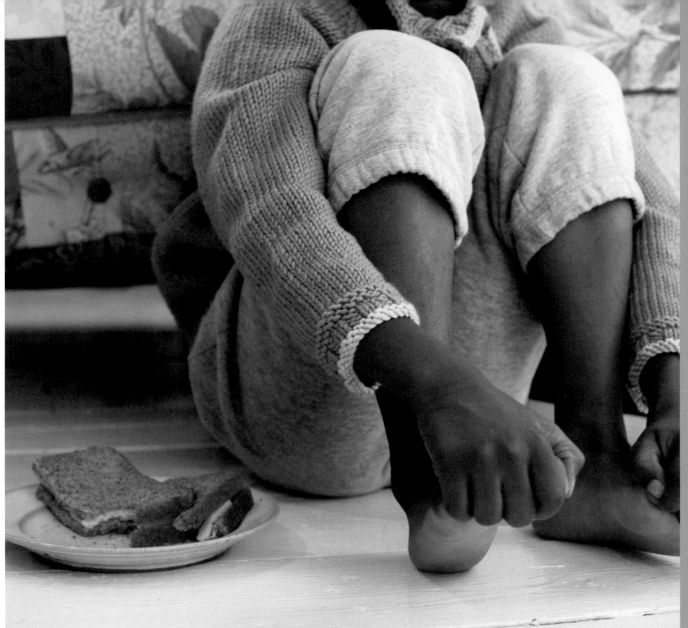

1st row (right side of collar, wrong side of sweater) P2, * k2, p2; rep from * to end.
2nd row K2, p2tog, yrn, rib 6, p2tog, yrn, rib to end.
3rd row As 1st row.
Change to C.
4th row K12, p18.
5th row P18, k12.
Cast off row Cast off 12 sts knitwise, then 18 sts purlwise.

to make up   Join side and sleeve seams. Lap buttonhole band over button band and sew in place. Sew on buttons.

measurements
Length approximately 106cm
Width approximately 106cm

materials
22 x 50g balls Debbie Bliss Cashmerino Aran in each of chocolate (A) and raspberry (B)
Long 5mm circular knitting needle

tension
18 sts and 30 rows to 10cm square over moss st using 5mm needles.

abbreviations
See page 23.

note
Use separate balls of yarn for side edging, twisting yarns on wrong side to avoid a hole.

tv blanket

first side

With 5mm circular needle and A, cast on 181 sts.
Work backwards and forwards in rows:
K 11 rows.
Foundation row With A, k5, with B, k to last 5 sts, with A, k5.
Patt row With A, k5, with B, k1, [p1, k1] 85 times, with A, k5.
Rep this row until blanket measures 103cm from cast-on edge, ending with a wrong side row.
With A, k 11 rows.
Cast off.

second side

Work as given for first side, reading B for A and A for B.

to make up

Join first and second sides together around the outer edge.

measurements

Size approximately 26cm tall

materials

1 x 50g ball Debbie Bliss Baby Cashmerino in each
of stone (A), white (B), jade (C), teal (D) and rose (E)
Pair 2³/₄mm knitting needles
Washable toy stuffing
50cm of narrow ribbon
1 small button

tension

24 sts and 40 rows to 10cm square over st st using
2³/₄mm needles.

rag doll 53

abbreviations

s2togkpo = slip next 2 sts tog, k1, then pass slipped
sts over so centre st lies on top.
ssk = [sl 1 knitwise] twice, insert tip of left-hand
needle from left to right through fronts of slipped
sts and k2tog.
Also see page 23.

note

All pieces for the doll and dress are made using
2³/₄mm needles.

body (worked from the neck edge)

With A, cast on 17 sts.

P 1 row.

Inc row (right side) K4, m1, k1, m1, k7, m1, k1, m1, k4. 21 sts.

Work 3 rows in st st.

Inc row K5, m1, k1, m1, k9, m1, k1, m1, k5. 25 sts.

Work 3 rows in st st.

Inc row K6, m1, k1, m1, k11, m1, k1, m1, k6. 29 sts.

Work 13 rows in st st.

Change to B and k 2 rows.

Beg with a k row, work 8 rows in st st.

Shape crotch and legs

Next row Ssk, k12, ssk, k11, k2tog. 26 sts.

Next row P13, turn and work on these sts only for left leg, leave rem 13 sts on a spare needle.

Beg with a k row, work 5 rows in st st.

K 1 row.

Beg with a k row, work in striped st st of [4 rows C, 4 rows D] 5 times, then 2 rows in C.

Cont in D only.

Shape foot

Next row K4, cast on 10 sts, k9. 23 sts.

Work 3 rows in st st.

Next row K8, m1, k2, m1, k13. 25 sts.

P 1 row.

Next row K8, m1, k4, m1, k13. 27 sts.

Work 2 rows in st st.

Next row (wrong side) Cast off 13 sts knitwise, k to end.

Next row Cast off 10, k to end. 4 sts.

Sole

Next row [Kfb, k1] twice. 6 sts.

K 1 row.

Next row Kfb, k3, kfb, k1. 8 sts.

K 8 rows.

Next row K2tog, k4, ssk. 6 sts.

K 1 row.

Next row K2tog, k2, ssk.

Cast off rem 4 sts.

With wrong side facing and B, rejoin yarn to 13 sts on spare needle, p to end.

Beg with a k row, work 5 rows in st st.

K 1 row.

Beg with a k row, work in striped st st of [4 rows C, 4 rows D] 4 times, then 2 rows in C.

Cont in D only.

Shape foot

Next row K9, cast on 10 sts, k4. 23 sts.

Work 3 rows in st st.

Next row K13, m1, k2, m1, k8. 25 sts.

P 1 row.
Next row K13, m1, k4, m1, k8. 27 sts.
Work 2 rows in st st.
Next row (wrong side) Cast off 10 sts knitwise, k to end.
Next row Cast off 13, k to end. 4 sts.
Sole
Next row [Kfb, k1] twice.
K 1 row.
Next row Kfb, k3, kfb, k1. 8 sts.
K 8 rows.
Next row K2tog, k4, ssk. 6 sts.
K 1 row.
Next row K2tog, k2, ssk.
Cast off rem 4 sts.

arms (worked from
hand to shoulder, make 2)

With A, cast on 5 sts.
P 1 row.
Next row K1, [m1, k1] 4 times. 9 sts.
P 1 row.
Next row K1, m1, k2, m1, k3, m1, k2, m1, k1. 13 sts.
Work 3 rows in st st.
Next row K1, ssk, k1, ssk, k1, k2tog, k1, k2tog, k1. 9 sts.
Beg with a p row, work 13 rows in st st.
Next row Ssk, k5, k2tog. 7 sts.
P 1 row.
Next row Ssk, k3, k2tog. 5 sts.
P 1 row.
Next row Ssk, k1, k2tog. 3 sts.
P 1 row.
Next row S2togkpo.

head

With A, cast on 9 sts.
Beg with a k row, work 2 rows in st st.
Next row K1, [m1, k1] 8 times. 17 sts.
P 1 row.
Next row [K2, m1] 4 times, k1, [m1, k2] 4 times. 25 sts.
P 1 row.
Next row K6, m1, k1, m1, k11, m1, k1, m1, k6. 29 sts.
Work 3 rows in st st.
Next row K7, m1, k1, m1, k13, m1, k1, m1, k7. 33 sts.
Work 5 rows in st st.
Next row K6, ssk, k1, k2tog, k11, ssk, k1, k2tog, k6. 29 sts.
Work 3 rows in st st.
Next row K5, ssk, k1, k2tog, k9, ssk, k1, k2tog, k5. 25 sts.

hair

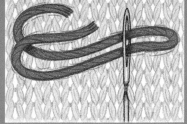

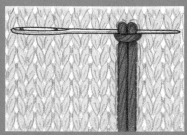

1 Thread a 13 cm loop of yarn through needle and insert point of the needle from top to bottom through bar in the centre of a stitch or between two stitches.
2 Pull yarn loop through then remove needle. Pass the two yarn ends through the loop.
3 Place needle under the double yarn above the loop and pull yarn ends to tighten loop onto yarn.

Repeat these steps working hair all over head, working as densely or sparsely as required. Trim yarn lengths into a hair style.

P 1 row.
Next row K2, [ssk, k1] twice, [ssk] twice, k1, [k2tog] twice, [k1, k2tog] twice, k2. **17 sts.**
P 1 row.
Next row K2, [ssk, k1] twice, k1, [k1, k2tog] twice, k2. **13 sts.**
P 1 row.
Next row K1, [ssk] twice, s2togkpo, [k2tog] twice, k1. **7 sts.**
Break yarn, thread through rem sts, pull up and secure.

to make up   Fold 10 cast-on sts of each foot in half and join to form top of shoe. Join leg and foot/shoe seams.
Sew soles in place. Stuff feet/shoes and legs. Join back and crotch seam leaving cast-on edge
open. Stuff body. Join arm seams leaving shaped top edge open. Stuff and sew to body using
side shapings as a guide to position. Join head seam. Sew head to neck edge. Attach lengths of
yarn to head for hair strands (see hair steps), and trim into your chosen style. Embroider a few
stitches on face for eyes and mouth.

dress   With E, cast on 55 sts.
K 1 row.
Beg with a k row, work in st st until dress measures 7.5cm ending with a p row.
Dec row K1, [k2tog, k1] to end. **37 sts.**
K 4 rows.
Next row (wrong side) K8, cast off 3 sts knitwise, k until there are 15 sts on right-hand needle,
cast off 3 sts knitwise, k to end.
Work on last group of 8 sts only for left back, leave rem groups of sts on a spare needle.
K 13 rows.
Cast off knitwise.
With right side facing, rejoin yarn to centre group of 15 sts for front and k 3 rows.
Next row (wrong side) K5, p5, k5.
K 1 row.
Rep the last 2 rows twice more.
K 4 rows.
Cast off knitwise.
With right side facing, rejoin yarn to last group of 8 sts for right back and k 13 rows.
Cast off knitwise.

to make up   Join 3 sts of left and right back to front for shoulders. Join back seam from cast-on edge to beg
of garter st yoke. Make a small button loop on edge of left back and sew button on right back to
match. Cut lengths of ribbon, thread through top of shoes and tie in a bow.

measurements
Length 48cm
Width 46cm

materials
For one cushion
7 x 50g balls Debbie Bliss Rialto Aran
in pale blue (A) or mulberry (B) and
1 x 50g ball in Debbie Bliss Rialto Aran
in mulberry (B) or pale blue (A)
Pair 5mm knitting needles

tension
18 sts and 24 rows to 10cm square
over st st using 5mm needles.

abbreviations
See page 23.

alphabet cushions

intarsia chart note
Use separate small balls of yarn for each colour area and twist yarns at colour change to avoid holes forming. Read right side (k) rows of chart from right to left and wrong side (p) rows of chart from left to right, noting that 1st chart row is a wrong side (p) row.

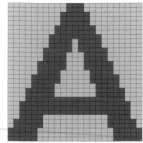
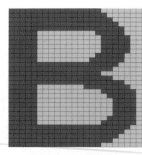
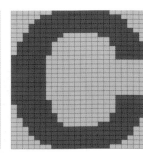

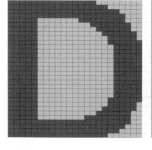
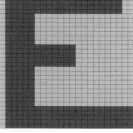
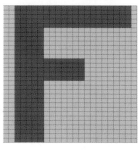
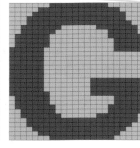
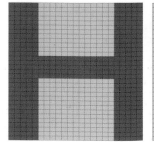
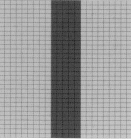
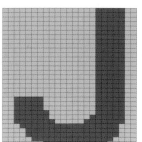
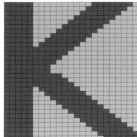

 A   ■ B   Each chart has 23 sts and 31 rows

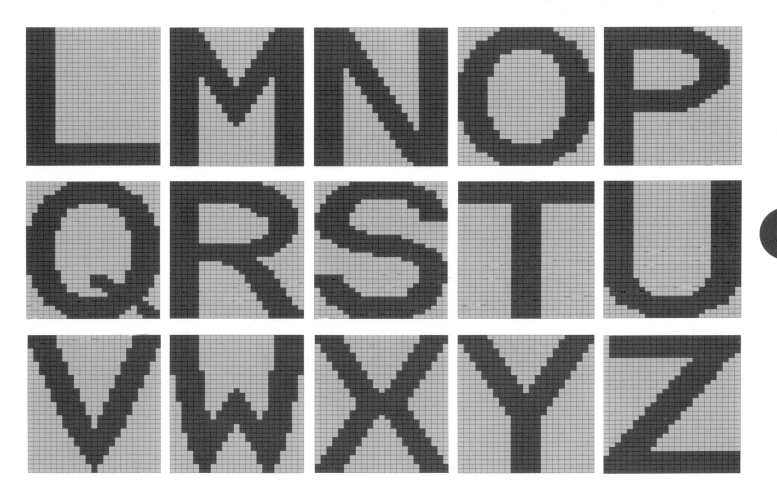

to make

With 5mm needles and A, cast on 83 sts.
Moss st row K1, [p1, k1] to end.
Rep the moss st row 5 times more.
Next row (right side) [K1, p1] 3 times, k71, [p1, k1] 3 times.
Next row [K1, p1] 3 times, p71, [p1, k1] 3 times.
Rep the last 2 rows 29 times more.
Moss st row K1, [p1, k1] to end.
Rep the moss st row 6 times more, so ending with a right side row.
P 3 rows, the 2nd of these 3 rows forms the ridge row.
Moss st row K1, [p1, k1] to end.
Rep the moss st row 6 times more, so ending with a right side row.
Next row [K1, p1] 3 times, p71, [p1, k1] 3 times.
Next row [K1, p1] 3 times, k71, [p1, k1] 3 times.
Rep the last 2 rows 16 times more.
Next row [K1, p1] 3 times, p24, p across 23 sts of 1st row of chart, p24, [p1, k1] 3 times.
Next row [K1, p1] 3 times, k24, k across 23 sts of 2nd row of chart, k24, [p1, k1] 3 times.
Rep the last 2 rows, working correct chart rows until chart is complete, so ending with a wrong side row.
Next row [K1, p1] 3 times, k71, [p1, k1] 3 times.
Next row [K1, p1] 3 times, p71, [p1, k1] 3 times.
Rep the last 2 rows 15 times more, then the 1st of these 2 rows again.
Moss st row K1, [p1, k1] to end.
Rep the moss st row 6 times more, so ending with a right side row.
P 3 rows, the 2nd of these 3 rows forms the ridge row.
Moss st row K1, [p1, k1] to end.
Rep the moss st row 6 times more, so ending with a right side row.
Next row [K1, p1] 3 times, p71, [p1, k1] 3 times.
Next row [K1, p1] 3 times, k71, [p1, k1] 3 times.
Rep the last 2 rows 29 times more.
Moss st row K1, [p1, k1] to end.
Rep the moss st row 6 times more.
Cast off in moss st.

to make up

Lightly press omitting moss st areas. Fold lower cushion back onto wrong side along ridge row and stitch back to cushion front along side edges. Fold upper cushion back onto wrong side along ridge row and stitch to cushion front along side edges, where it overlaps onto lower back, stitch through all thicknesses.

measurements
To fit ages 2–3 (3–4: 4–5) years
actual measurements
Chest 70 (76: 82)cm
Length to shoulder 33 (37: 41)cm

materials
6 (7: 7) x 50g balls Debbie Bliss Rialto Aran in stone
Pair each 4¹/₂mm and 5mm knitting needles
35 (40: 45)cm open-ended zip

tension
18 sts and 24 rows to 10cm square over st st using 5mm needles.

abbreviations
See page 23.

zippedgilet

back

With 4¹/₂mm needles, cast on 66 (70: 74) sts.
1st and 3rd sizes only
1st row (right side) P2, [k2, p2] to end.
2nd row P to end.
2nd size only
1st row (right side) K2, [p2, k2] to end.
2nd row P to end.
All sizes
Rep the last 2 rows 3 times more.
Change to 5mm needles.
Beg with a k row, work in st st until back measures 21 (24: 27)cm from cast-on edge, ending with
a p row.
Shape armholes
Cast off 6 sts at beg of next 2 rows. 54 (58: 62) sts.
Cont in patt until work measures 33 (37: 41)cm from cast-on edge, ending with a p row.
Shape shoulders
Cast off 15 (16: 17) sts at beg of next 2 rows.
Leave rem 24 (26: 28) sts on a spare needle.

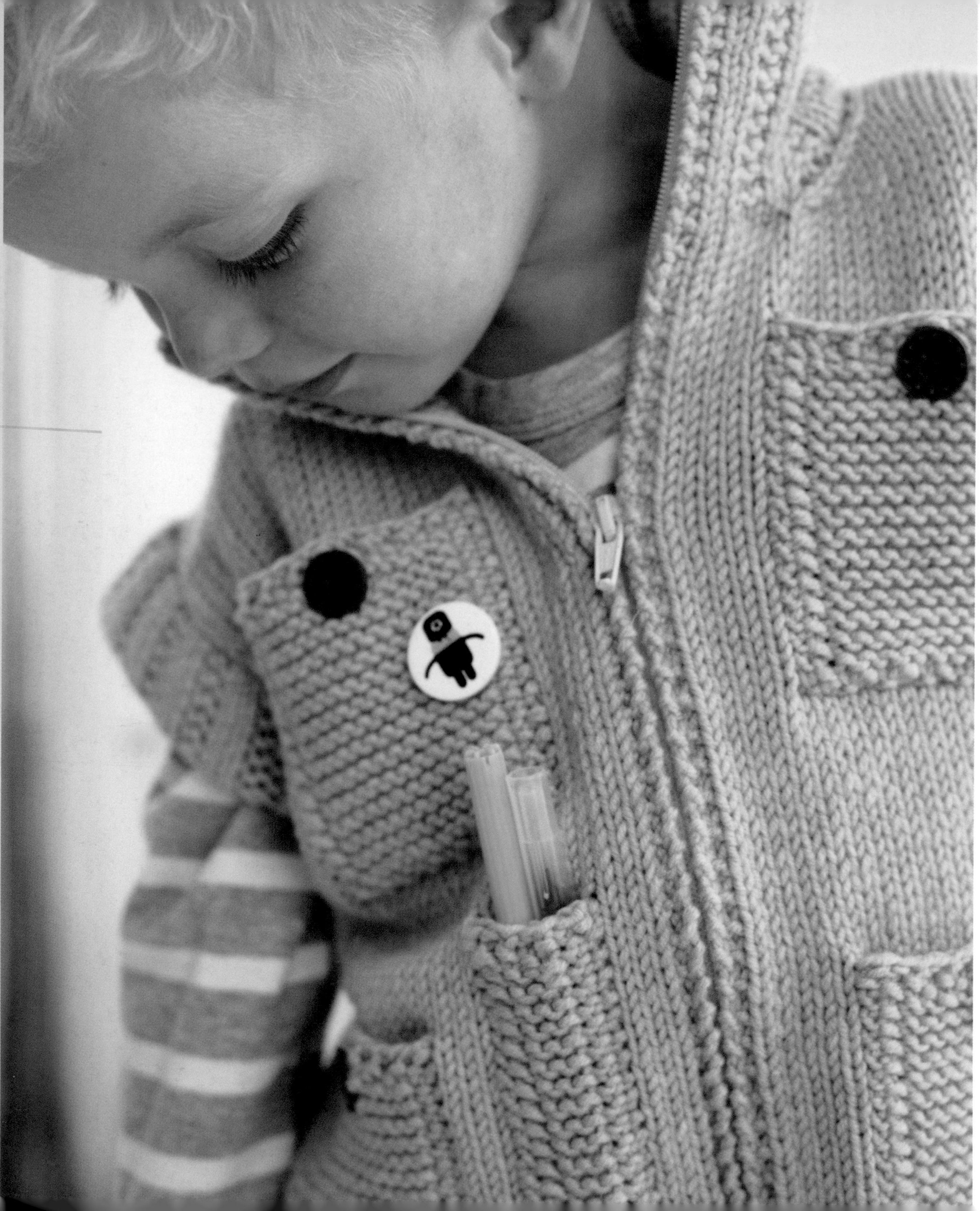

left front

With 4¹/₂mm needles, cast on 34 (36: 38) sts.

1st and 3rd sizes only

1st row (right side) P2, [k2, p2] to last 4 sts, k4.

2nd row K2, p to end.

2nd size only

1st row (right side) [K2, p2] to last 4 sts, k4.

2nd row K2, p to end.

All sizes

Rep the last 2 rows 3 times more.

Change to 5mm needles.

Next row (right side) K to end.

Next row K2, p to end.

These 2 rows form the st st with garter st front edging.

Cont straight until front measures 21 (24: 27)cm from cast-on edge, ending with a wrong side row.

Shape armhole

Next row Cast off 6 sts, k to end. 28 (30: 32) sts.

Work straight until front measures 29 (33: 37)cm from cast-on edge, ending with a wrong side row.

Shape neck

Next row (right side) K22 (23: 24) sts, turn and work on these sts only for first side of neck, leave rem 6 (7: 8) sts on a holder.

Dec 1 st at neck edge on next 7 rows. 15 (16: 17) sts.

Work straight until front matches Back to shoulder, ending at armhole edge.

Shape shoulder

Cast off.

right front

With 4¹/₂mm needles, cast on 34 (36: 38) sts.

1st and 3rd sizes only

1st row (right side) K4, p2, [k2, p2] to end.

2nd row P to last 2 sts, k2.

2nd size only

1st row (right side) K4, [p2, k2] to end.

2nd row P to last 2 sts, k2.

All sizes

Rep the last 2 rows 3 times more.

Change to 5mm needles.

Next row (right side) K to end.

Next row P to last 2 sts, k2.

These 2 rows form the st st with garter st front edging.

Cont straight until front measures 21 (24: 27)cm from cast-on edge, ending with a right side row.

Shape armhole

Next row Cast off 6 sts, p to last 2 sts, k2. 28 (30: 32) sts.

Work straight until front measures 29 (33: 37)cm from cast-on edge, ending with a wrong side row.

Shape neck

Next row (right side) K6 (7: 8) sts, slip these sts onto a holder, k to end. 22 (23: 24) sts.

Dec 1 st at neck edge on next 7 rows. 15 (16: 17) sts
Work straight until front matches Back to shoulder shaping, ending at armhole edge.
Shape shoulder
Cast off.

collar

Join shoulder seams.
With right side facing and 4 1/2 mm needles, slip 6 (7: 8) sts from right front onto a needle, pick up and k9 sts up right side of front neck, k24 (26: 28) sts from back neck, pick up and k9 sts down left side of front neck, then k6 (7: 8) sts from left front holder. 54 (58: 62) sts.
1st rib row (wrong side) K2, p to last 2 sts, k2.
2nd rib row K4, [p2, k2] to last 6 sts, p2, k4.
These 2 rows form the patt and are repeated throughout.
Work a further 6 (7: 8)cm in patt, ending with a wrong side row.
Next row (right side) K4, [p2, k2] to last 6 sts, p2, k4.
Next row K2, [p2, k2] to end.
Rep the last 2 rows until collar measures 12 (14: 16)cm, ending with a wrong side row.
Cast off in rib.

armbands

With right side facing and 4 1/2 mm needles, pick up and k50 (54: 58) sts evenly along armhole edge.
1st rib row (wrong side) P to end.
2nd rib row K2, [p2, k2] to end.
Rep the last 2 rows 5 times more.
Next row P2, [k2, p2] to end.
Next row K2, [p2, k2] to end.
Rep the last 2 rows 4 times more and the first row again.
Cast off in rib.

pockets (make 4)

With 4 1/2 mm needles, cast on 15 (17: 19) sts.
1st row (wrong side) K1, [p1, k1] to end.
2nd row As 1st row.
3rd row K1, p1, k11 (13: 15), p1, k1.
Rep the last row until pocket measures 7 (8: 9)cm from cast-on edge, ending with a wrong side row.
1st buttonhole row K1, p1, k4 (5: 6), k2tog, yf, k5 (6: 7), p1, k1.
3rd row K1, p1, k(11: 13: 15), p1, k1.
Next row K1, * p1, k1; rep from * to end.
Rep the last row once more.
Cast off in patt.

slim pocket (make 1)

With 4 1/2 mm needles, cast on 7 sts.
1st row (wrong side) K1, [p1, k1] to end.
2nd row As 1st row.
3rd row K1, p1, k3, p1, k1.
Rep the last row until pocket measures 10 (11: 12)cm from cast-on edge, ending with a wrong side row.
Next row K1, [p1, k1] to end.

Rep the last row once more.
Cast off in patt.

to make up   Sew first 8 row-ends of armbands to sts cast off at underarm. Join side and armband seams,
leaving last 8 rows of armbands unstitched. Fold armbands in half onto wrong side and slipstitch
in place. Hand-sew zip in place behind front edging, from halfway along collar edge to cast-on
edge. Fold collar in half onto wrong side and slip stitch in place. Sew on pockets. Sew on buttons.

special time

measurements
To fit ages 2–3 (3–4: 4–5) years
actual measurements
Chest 59 (65: 71)cm
Length to shoulder 31 (34: 37)cm
Sleeve length 22 (25: 28)cm

materials
5 (6: 6) x 50g balls Debbie Bliss Baby Cashmerino in pale pink (M) and 1 x 50g ball in each of
mid green (A), pale green (B), ecru (C), mid pink (D), lemon (E) and chocolate (F)
Pair each 2^3/$_4$mm and 3^1/$_4$mm knitting needles
3 buttons
1.5m narrow ribbon

tension
25 sts and 34 rows over st st and 27 sts and 34 rows over Fairisle st st to 10cm square both using
3^1/$_4$mm needles.

fairisle jacket

back

With 2^3/$_4$mm needles and M, cast on 101 (111· 121) sts.
K 3 rows.
Change to 3^1/$_4$mm needles.
Beg with a k row, work in st st until back measures 16 (19: 22)cm from cast-on edge, ending with a k row.
Dec row (wrong side) P2, [p2tog, p3] 19 (21: 23) times, p2tog, p2. 81 (89: 97) sts.
Now work in st st from Chart until back measures 19 (21: 23)cm from cast-on edge, ending with a p row.
Shape armholes
Cast off 4 sts at beg of next 2 rows. 73 (81: 89) sts.
Dec 1 st at each end of next row and 3 (4: 5) foll right side rows. 65 (71: 77) sts.
Cont straight until all 36 chart rows have been worked, then cont in M only until back measures
31 (34: 37)cm from cast-on edge, ending with a p row.
Shape shoulders
Cast off 13 (15: 17) sts at beg of next 2 rows.
Leave rem 39 (41: 43) sts on a holder.

left front

** With 2^3/$_4$mm needles and M, cast on 51 (56: 61) sts.
K 3 rows.
Change to 3^1/$_4$mm needles.
Beg with a k row, work in st st until front measures 16 (19: 22)cm from cast-on edge, ending with a k row.
Dec row (wrong side) P2, [p2tog, p3] 9 (10: 11) times, p2tog, p2. 41 (45: 49) sts. **

Now work in st st from Chart until front measures 19 (21: 23)cm from cast-on edge, ending with a p row.
Shape armhole
Cast off 4 sts at beg of next row. 37 (41: 45) sts.
Next row Patt to end.
Dec 1 st at beg of next row and 3 (4: 5) foll right side rows. 33 (36: 39) sts.
Cont straight until front measures 24 (26: 29)cm from cast-on edge, ending with a p row.
Shape neck
Next row (right side) Patt to last 6 (7: 8) sts, leave these sts on a holder and cont on rem 27 (29: 31) sts.
Dec 1 st at neck edge on every row until 13 (15: 17) sts rem, **at the same time**, when all 36 chart rows have been worked, cont in M only until front measures same as Back to shoulder, ending at armhole edge.
Shape shoulder
Cast off.

right front

Work exactly as for Left Front from ** to **.
Now work in st st from Chart until front measures 19 (21: 23)cm from cast-on edge, ending with a k row.
Shape armhole
Cast off 4 sts at beg of next row. 37 (41: 45) sts.
Dec 1 st at end of the next and 3 (4: 5) foll right side rows. 33 (36: 39) sts.
Cont straight until front measures 24 (26: 29)cm from cast-on edge, ending with a p row.
Shape neck
Next row Patt 6 (7: 8) sts, leave these sts on a holder, patt to end and cont on rem 27 (29: 31) sts.
Dec 1 st at neck edge on every row until 13 (15: 17) sts rem, **at the same time**, when all 36 chart rows have been worked, cont in M only until front measures same as Back to shoulder, ending at armhole edge.
Shape shoulder
Cast off.

sleeves

With 2³/₄mm needles and M, cast on 41 (45: 49) sts.
K 3 rows.
Change to 3¹/₄mm needles.
Beg with a k row, work 2 rows in st st.
Work Chart rows 33 to 36, as given for Left Front.
Cont in M only.
Inc 1 st at each end of next row and every foll 6th row until there are 61 (69: 75) sts.
Cont straight until sleeve measures 22 (25: 28)cm from cast-on edge, ending with a p row.
Shape top
Cast off 4 sts at beg of next 2 rows. 53 (61: 67) sts.
Next row K2, skpo, k to last 4 sts, k2tog, k2.
Next row P to end.
Rep the last 2 rows 3 (4: 5) times more. 45 (51: 55) sts.
Cast off 3 sts at beg of next 12 rows.
Cast off rem 9 (15: 19) sts.

2nd size left front
2nd size right front

8 st patt rep

all sizes back, 1st and 3rd sizes left and right front

| M pale pink | A mid green | B pale green | C ecru | D mid pink | E lemon | F chocolate |

neckband

With right side facing, $2^3/_4$mm needles and M, slip 6 (7: 8) sts from right front neck holder onto a needle, pick up and k24 (26: 26) sts up right front neck, k39 (41: 43) sts from back neck holder, pick up and k24 (26: 26) sts down left side of front neck, k 6 (7: 8) sts from left front holder. 99 (107: 111) sts.
K 3 rows.
Cast off.

button band

With right side facing, $2^3/_4$mm needles and M, pick up and k64 (68: 72) sts along left front edge.
K 3 rows.
Cast off.

buttonhole band

With right side facing, $2^3/_4$mm needles and M, pick up and k64 (68: 72) sts along right front edge.
K 1 row.
Buttonhole row K38 (40: 42), [k2tog, yf, k8 (9: 10)] twice, k2tog, yf, k4.
K 1 row. Cast off.

to make up

Sew sleeves into armholes, easing to fit. Join side and sleeve seams. Sew on buttons. Thread ribbon through cardigan, just below beg of fairisle yoke.

measurements

To fit ages 2–3 (3–4: 4–5) years

actual measurements

Chest 31 (38: 45)cm
Length to shoulder 17 (19: 21)cm
Sleeve length 17 (19: 21)cm

materials

3 (4: 4) x 50g balls Debbie Bliss
Cashmerino Aran in jade
Pair each 4^1/$_2$mm and 5mm knitting
needles

tension

18 sts and 24 rows to 10cm square
over st st using 5mm needles.

abbreviations

See page 23.

party shrug

left sleeve

With 4½mm needles, cast on 34 (38: 42) sts.
K 3 rows.
Change to 5mm needles.
Beg with a k row, work in st st.
Work 2 rows.
Next row K3, m1, k to last 3 sts, m1, k3.
Work 5 rows.
Rep the last 6 rows until there are 46 (52: 58) sts.
Cont straight until sleeve measures 17 (19: 21)cm from cast-on edge, ending with a p row **.
Shape top
Next row Cast on 4 (5: 6) sts, k to end.
Next row Cast on 4 (5: 6) sts, p to end. 54 (62: 70) sts
Next row K3, skpo, k to end.
Next row P to last 5 sts, p2tog tbl, p3.
Rep the last 2 rows 10 (11: 12) times more. 32 (38: 44) sts.
Next row K3, skpo, k to end.
Next row P to end.
Rep the last 2 rows 4 (6: 8) times more. 27 (31: 35) sts.
Work 6 (8: 10) rows straight.
Cast off.

right sleeve

Work as given for Left Sleeve to **.
Shape top
Next row Cast on 4 (5: 6) sts, k to end.
Next row Cast on 4 (5: 6) sts, p to end. 54 (62: 70) sts
Next row K to last 5 sts, k2tog, k3.
Next row P3, p2tog, p to end.
Rep the last 2 rows 10 (11: 12) times more. 32 (38: 44) sts.
Next row K to last 5 sts, k2tog, k3.
Next row P to end.
Rep the last 2 rows 4 (6: 8) times more. 27 (31: 35) sts.
Work 6 (8: 10) rows straight.
Cast off.

lower back border

Join back seam.
With right side facing and 4½mm needles, pick up and k62 (66: 70) sts along row ends.
1st row P2, * k2, p2; rep from * to end.
2nd row K2, * p2, k2; rep from * to end.
Rep the last 2 rows twice more and the first row again.
Cast off in rib.

front and neck border

With right side facing and 4½mm needles, pick up and k35 (39: 43) sts along shaped edge, then
12 (16: 20) sts along straight row ends, then 35 (39: 43) sts along shaped edge. 82 (94: 106) sts.
1st row P2, * k2, p2; rep from * to end.

This row sets the rib.
Next 2 rows Rib to last 30 (36: 42) sts, turn.
Next 2 rows Rib to last 24 (28: 32) sts, turn.
Next 2 rows Rib to last 18 (20: 22) sts, turn.
Next 2 rows Rib to last 12 sts, turn.
Next 2 rows Rib to last 6 sts, turn.
Rib to end.
Work 5 more rows in rib across all sts.
Cast off loosely in rib.

to make up   Join sleeve, side and border seams.

80 polo shirt

measurements

To fit ages 2–3 (3–4: 4–5) years

actual measurements

Chest 69 (75: 81)cm

Length to shoulder 33 (38: 43)cm

Sleeve length 22 (25: 28)cm

materials

5 (6: 7) x 50g balls Debbie Bliss Baby Cashmerino in black

Pair each $2^3/_4$mm and $3^1/_4$mm knitting needles

3 buttons

tension

25 sts and 34 rows to 10cm square over st st using $3^1/_4$mm needles.

abbreviations

See page 23.

back

With 2³/₄mm needles, cast on 88 (96: 104) sts.
1st rib row [K1, p1] to end.
This row forms the rib and is repeated.
Work a further 9 (11: 13) rib rows.
Change to 3¹/₄mm needles.
Beg with a k row, work in st st until back measures 21 (25: 29)cm from cast-on edge, ending with a p row.
Shape armholes
Cast off 6 (7: 8) sts at beg of next 2 rows. 76 (82: 88) sts. **
Next row K3, skpo, k to last 5 sts, k2tog, k3.
Next row P to end.
Rep the last 2 rows 6 (7: 8) times more. 62 (66: 70) sts.
Work straight until back measures 33 (38: 43)cm from cast-on edge, ending with a p row.
Shape shoulders
Cast off 9 (9: 10) sts at beg of next 2 rows and 9 (10: 10) sts on foll 2 rows.
Cast off rem 26 (28: 30) sts.

front

Work as given for Back to **.
Divide for front opening
Next row (right side) K3, skpo, k30 (33: 36), turn and work on these 34 (37: 40) sts only for first side of front neck, leave rem sts on a holder.
Next row P to end.
Next row K3, skpo, k to end.
Rep the last 2 rows 5 (6: 7) times more. 28 (30: 32) sts.
Work straight until front measures 29 (33: 37)cm from cast-on edge, ending with a p row.
Shape neck
Next row K to last 7 (8: 9) sts, turn and work on these 21 (22: 23) sts only, leave rem 7 (8: 9) sts on a holder.
Dec 1 st at neck edge on next 3 rows. 18 (19: 20) sts.
Work straight until front measures same as Back to shoulder, ending at armhole edge.
Shape shoulder
Cast off 9 (9: 10) sts at beg of next row. Work 1 row.
Cast off rem 9 (10: 10) sts.
With right side facing, join on yarn, cast off centre 6 sts, k to last 5 sts, k2tog, k3.
Next row P to end.
Next row K to last 5 sts, k2tog, k3.
Rep the last 2 rows 5 (6: 7) times more. 28 (30: 32) sts.
Work straight until front measures 29 (33: 37)cm from cast-on edge, ending with a p row.
Shape neck
Next row K 7 (8: 9) sts, leave these sts on a holder, k to end. 21 (22: 23) sts.
Dec 1 st at neck edge on next 3 rows. 18 (19: 20) sts.
Work straight until front measures same as Back to shoulder, ending at armhole edge.
Shape shoulder
Cast off 9 (9: 10) sts at beg of next row. Work 1 row.
Cast off rem 9 (10: 10) sts.

sleeves

With 2¾mm needles, cast on 50 (56: 62) sts.
1st rib row [K1, p1] to end.
This row forms the rib.
Work a further 15 rib rows.
Change to 3¼mm needles.
Beg with a k row, work 4 rows in st st.
Inc row K3, m1, k to last 3 sts, m1, k3.
Work 5 rows.
Rep the last 6 rows 7 (8: 9) times more and the inc row again. 68 (76: 84) sts.
Cont straight until sleeve measures 22 (25: 28)cm from cast-on edge, ending with a p row.
Shape sleeve top
Cast off 6 (7: 8) sts at beg of next 2 rows. 56 (62: 68) sts.
Next row K3, skpo, k to last 5 sts, k2tog, k3.
Next row P to end.
Rep the last 2 rows 6 (7: 8) times more. 42 (46: 50) sts.
Cast off.

button band

With right side facing and 2¾mm needles, pick up and k27 (29: 31) sts evenly along right front edge to beg of neck shaping.
1st rib row K1, [p1, k1] to end.
2nd rib row P1, [k1, p1] to end.
Rep the last 2 rows 3 times more and the 1st row again.
Cast off in rib.

buttonhole band

With right side facing and 2¾mm needles, pick up and k27 (29: 31) sts evenly along left front edge.
1st row K1, [p1, k1] to end.
2nd row P1, [k1, p1] to end.
Rep the last 2 rows once more.
Buttonhole row Rib 3, [yrn, rib 2tog, rib 7 (8: 9)] twice, yrn, rib 2tog, rib 4.
Rib 4 rows.
Cast off in rib.

collar

With 2¾mm needles cast on 39 (45: 51) sts.
Rib row K1, [p1, k1] to end.
Next row Cast on 6 sts, [p1, k1] 3 times across these sts, then rib to end.
Next row Cast on 6 sts, [k1, p1] 3 times across these sts, then rib to end.
Rep the last 2 rows 4 times more. 99 (105: 111) sts.
Change to 3¼mm needles.
Cont straight in rib until collar measures 9cm from cast-on edge.
Cast off in rib.

to make up

Sew sleeves into armholes easing to fit. Join side and sleeve seams. Place lower edge of left front band over lower edge of right front band and sew in place. Starting and ending halfway across front bands, sew cast-on edge of collar to neck edge.

smock dress

measurements
To fit ages 2–3 (3–4: 4–5) years
actual measurements
Chest 65 (71: 77)cm
Length to shoulder 50 (56: 64)cm
Sleeve length 22 (25: 28)cm

materials
7 (8: 9) x 50g balls Debbie Bliss Baby Cashmerino in silver
Pair each 2^3/$_4$mm and 3^1/$_4$mm knitting needles
2^3/$_4$mm circular knitting needle
4 buttons

tension
25 sts and 34 rows to 10cm square over st st using 3^1/$_4$mm needles.

abbreviations
See page 23.

back

With 2³/₄mm needles, cast on 110 (120: 130) sts.

K 5 rows.

Change to to 3¹/₄mm needles.

Beg with a k row, work in st st until back measures 35 (39: 45)cm from cast-on edge, ending with a k row.

Dec row (wrong side) P2 (3: 4), [p2tog, p2] 26 (28: 30) times, p2tog, p2 (3: 4). 83 (91: 99) sts **.

Change to 2³/₄mm needles.

Work in garter st (k every row) until back measures 38 (43: 50)cm from cast-on edge, ending with a wrong side row.

Shape armholes

Cast off 5 (6: 7) sts at beg of next 2 rows. 73 (79: 85) sts.

Next row K2, skpo, k to last 4 sts, k2tog, k2.

Next row K to end.

Rep the last 2 rows 7 (8: 9) times more. 57 (61: 65) sts rem.

Cont in garter st until back measures 50 (56: 64)cm from cast-on edge, ending with a wrong side row.

Shape shoulders

Cast off 13 (14: 15) sts at the beg of next 2 rows. 31 (33: 35) sts.

Cast off.

front

Work as given for Back to **.

Change to 2³/₄mm needles.

Front opening

Next row (right side) K38 (42: 46), turn and cont on these sts only, leave rem sts on a holder.

Next row Cast on 7 sts, k these 7 sts, k to end. 45 (49: 53) sts.

Cont in garter st until front measures 38 (43: 50)cm from cast-on edge, ending with a wrong side row.

Shape armhole

Cast off 5 (6: 7) sts at beg of next row. 40 (43: 46) sts.

K 1 row.

Next row K2, skpo, k to end.

Next row K to end.

Rep the last 2 rows 7 (8: 9) times more. 32 (34: 36) sts.

Cont in garter st until front measures 45 (50: 58)cm from cast-on edge, ending with a right side row.

Shape neck

Next row (wrong side) Cast off 13 (14: 15) sts, k to end.

Next row K to last 4 sts, k2tog, k2.

Next row K to end.

Rep the last 2 rows until 13 (14: 15) sts rem.

Work straight until left front measures same as Back to shoulder shaping, ending at armhole edge.

Shape shoulder

Cast off.

Mark position for 2 buttons the first 2 (3: 4)cm above opening, the second 2cm below neck shaping.

With right side facing, rejoin yarn to rem 45 (49: 53) sts, k to end.

Cont in garter st until front measures 37 (42: 49)cm from cast-on edge, ending with a wrong side row.

Buttonhole row K2, cast off 3 sts, k to end.

Next row K to end, casting on 3 sts over sts cast off in previous row.
Cont in garter st until front measures 38 (43: 50)cm from cast-on edge, ending with a right side row.
Shape armhole
Cast off 5 (6: 7) sts at beg of next row. 40 (43: 46) sts.
Next row K to last 4 sts, k2tog, k2.
Next row K to end.
Rep the last 2 rows 7 (8: 9) times more. 32 (34: 36) sts.
Cont straight in garter st, working 2nd buttonhole to match first when right front measures
43 (48: 56)cm, then cont in garter st until right front measures 45 (50: 58)cm from cast-on edge,
ending with a wrong side row.
Shape neck
Next row (right side) Cast off 13 (14: 15) sts, k to end.
K 1 row.
Next row K2, skpo, k to end.
Next row K to end.
Rep the last 2 rows until 13 (14: 15) sts rem.
Work straight until right front measures same as Back to shoulder shaping, ending at armhole edge.
Shape shoulder
Cast off.

sleeves

With 2³/₄mm needles, cast on 40 (44: 48) sts.
K 5 rows.
Change to 3¹/₄mm needles
Beg with a k row, work in st st and inc one st at each end of the 5th row and every foll 6th row
until there are 60 (68: 74) sts.
Cont straight until sleeve measures 22 (25: 28)cm from cast-on edge, ending with a p row.
Shape top
Cast off 4 (5: 6) sts at beg of next 2 rows. 52 (58: 62) sts.
Next row K2, skpo, k to last 4 sts, k2tog, k2.
Next row P to end.
Rep the last 2 rows 3 (4: 5) times more. 44 (48: 50) sts.
Cast off 3 sts at beg of next 12 rows.
Cast off rem 8 (12: 14) sts.

pockets

With 3¹/₄mm needles, cast on 19 (23: 27) sts.
Beg with a k row work 8 (9: 10)cm in st st, ending with a k row.
Change to 2³/₄mm needles.
K 3 rows.
Buttonhole row (right side) K8 (10: 12), cast off 3 sts, k to end.
Next row K to end, casting on 3 sts over those cast off in previous row.
K 2 rows.
Cast off.

to make up

Join side and sleeve seams. Sew sleeves into armholes easing to fit. Sew on pockets. Sew on buttons.

stripedtie

measurements
Length 21cm
Width 4cm

materials
1 x 50g ball Debbie Bliss Cashmerino DK in each of black (A) and yellow (B)
Pair 4mm knitting needles
30cm (or neck length) of 12mm wide elastic
Small piece of black Velcro™

tension
22 st and 30 rows to 10cm square over st st using 4mm needles.

abbreviations
ssk = [sl 1 knitwise] twice, insert tip of left-hand needle from left to right through fronts of slipped sts and k2tog.
Also see page 23.

main section

With 4mm needles and A, cast on 18 sts.
Beg with a k row, work 3 rows in st st.
Beg with a p row, work 4 rows st st in B, then 4 rows in A.
Rep the last 8 rows 3 times more.
Work 4 rows in B.
P 1 row in A.
Dec row With A, k1, ssk, k to last 3 sts, k2tog, k1.
Rep the last 2 rows once more.
P 1 row in B.
Dec row With B, k1, ssk, k to last 3 sts, k2tog, k1. 12 sts.
Work 2 rows in B.
Beg with a p row, work 4 rows st st in A.
P 1 row in B.
Inc row With B, k2, m1, k to last 2 sts, m1, k2. 14 sts.
Work 2 rows in B.
P 1 row in A.
Inc row With A, k2, m1, k to last 2 sts, m1, k2. 16 sts.
Work 2 rows in A.
Work 4 rows in B.
Work 3 rows in A.
Dec row With A, k1, ssk, k to last 3 sts, k2tog, k1. 14 sts.
Work 3 rows in B.
Dec row With B, k1, ssk, k to last 3 sts, k2tog, k1. 12 sts.
Work 4 rows in A.
Work 3 rows in B.
Inc row With B, k2, m1, k to last 2 sts, m1, k2. 14 sts.
P 1 row in A.
Inc row With A, k2, m1, k to last 2 sts, m1, k2. 16 sts.
P 1 row in A.
Inc row With A, k2, m1, k to last 2 sts, m1, k2. 18 sts.
Beg with a p row, work 4 rows st st in B, then 4 rows in A.
Rep the last 8 rows 3 times more.
Work 4 rows in B.
Work 3 rows in A.
Cast off in A.

neck strip

With 4mm needles and A, cast on 9 sts.
Beg with a k row, work in st st until strip measures 8cm, ending with a p row. Cast off.

to make up

Fold main part in half lengthwise and taking a half stitch from each edge and matching stripes, join seam using mattress stitch. Refold so that seam runs centrally and stitch across the ends. Join neck strip in the same way, leaving ends open. Insert the elastic into the neck strip, so strip lies centrally and stitch to secure. Fold main part in half over the neck strip and stitch through all layers to form the 'knot'. Sew small pieces of Velcro™ to the ends of elastic.

beaded bag

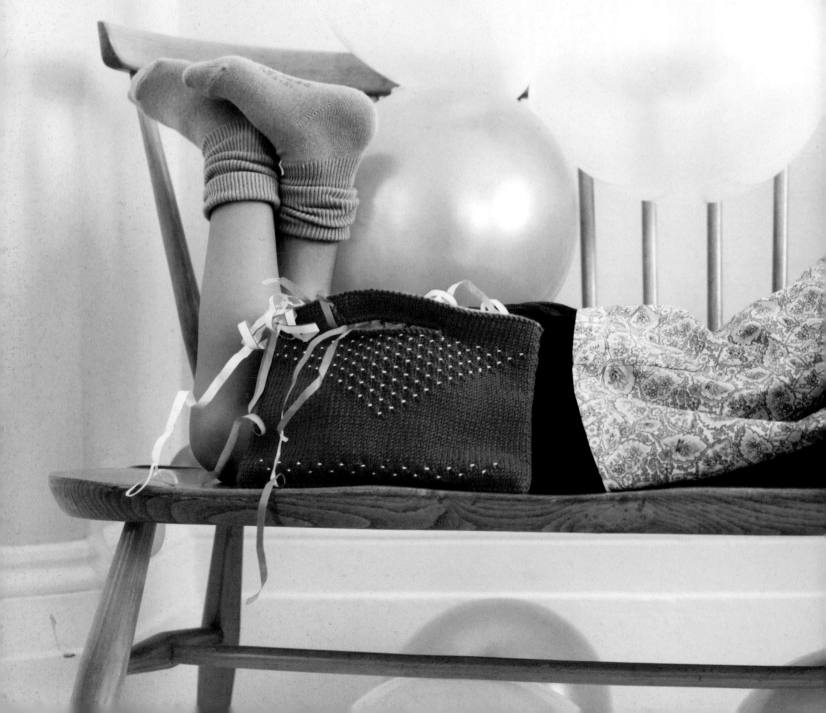

measurements
Height 16cm
Width 22cm

materials
1 x 50g ball Debbie Bliss Baby Cashmerino in old rose
(A) and pale jade (B)
Pair 3¹/₄mm knitting needles
Approximately 260 small glass beads with a silver
core – we used 1 x 25g pack of SB7 colour 1 (silver)
embroidery beads, available from creativebeadcraft.co.uk
Fine sewing needle and short length of sewing thread

tension
25 st and 34 rows to 10cm square over st st using
3¹/₄mm needles.

abbreviations
B(b)1 = bead 1 st by bringing yarn to front of work,
slide bead into position, p1, then take yarn to back of
work to k next st.
ssk = [sl 1 knitwise] twice, insert tip of left-hand needle
through fronts of slipped sts and k2tog.
Also see page 23.

note

The bag and lining are worked in one piece, from the base of the inner bag back, to the base of the inner bag front.

If substituting beads, check before buying that they have a central hole large enough for a double thickness of yarn to pass through.

You will need 256 beads for the bag. Thread beads onto yarn before starting, threading on a few more beads than are strictly necessary, in case of mistakes or damage. Remove damaged or misplaced beads on completion by breaking with a pair of pliers.

to make

Inner bag back

With 3¼mm needles and B, cast on 55 sts.

Beg with a k row, work 45 rows in st st, so ending with a k row.

Next row (wrong side) P17, cast off next 21 sts knitwise, p to end.

Next row K17, cast on 21 sts, k to end. 55 sts.

Beg with a p row, work 6 rows in st st.

Inc row P1, m1, p to last st, p1, k1. 57 sts.

Outer bag back

Change to A and k 1 row.

Ridge row (wrong side) K.

Beg with a k row, work 7 rows in st st.

Next row P18, cast off next 21 sts knitwise, p to end.

Next row K18, cast on 21 sts, k to end.

P 1 row.

Beg with a k row, work 47 rows from beading chart 1, so ending with a k row.

Base ridge row (wrong side) K.

Outer bag front

Beg with a k row, work 47 rows from beading chart 2, so ending with a k row.

P 1 row.

Next row K18, cast off next 21 sts purlwise, k to end.

Next row P18, cast on 21 sts, p to end.

Beg with a k row, work 7 rows in st st.

Ridge row (wrong side) K.

Inner bag front

Change to B.

Dec row Ssk, k to last 2 sts, k2tog. 55 sts.

Beg with a p row, work 6 rows in st st.

Next row (wrong side) P17, cast off next 21 sts knitwise, p to end.

Next row K17, cast on 21 sts, k to end.

Beg with a p row, work 45 rows in st st, so ending with a p row.

Cast off.

to make up

Join cast-on and cast-off edges to form base of inner bag. Join inner bag edges. Fold outer bag along base ridge row, join sides of outer bag, then slipstitch inner to outer bag around edges of handle openings.

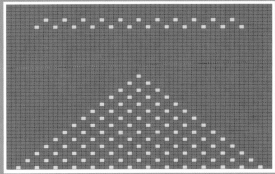

chart 1

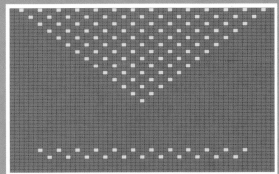

chart 2

B1 bead one stitch (see abbreviations for full explanation)

pea jacket

measurements
To fit ages 2–3 (3–4: 4–5) years
actual measurements
Chest 78 (83: 87)cm
Length to shoulder 40 (44: 48)cm
Sleeve length with cuff turned back 24 (27: 30)cm

materials
9 (10: 11) x 50g balls Debbie Bliss Rialto Aran in stone (M)
1 (1: 1) x 50g ball Debbie Bliss Rialto Aran in navy (C)
Pair each 4$^1/_2$mm and 5mm knitting needles
Set of 4$^1/_2$mm double-pointed needles
6 buttons

tension
18 sts and 30 rows to 10cm square over moss st using 5mm needles.

abbreviations
See page 23.

back

With 4½mm needles and C, cast on 71 (75: 79) sts.

K 1 row.

Change to 5mm needles and cont in M only.

Next row (right side) K to end.

Moss st row K1, [p1, k1] to end.

This row forms the moss st.

Cont in moss st until back measures 27 (30: 33)cm from cast-on edge, ending with a wrong side row.

Shape armholes

Cast off 6 sts at beg of next 2 rows. 59 (63: 67) sts.

Cont straight until back measures 40 (44: 48)cm from cast-on edge, ending with a wrong side row.

Shape shoulders

Cast off 10 (10: 11) sts at beg of next 2 rows and 9 (10: 10) sts at beg of foll 2 rows.

Cast off rem 21 (23: 25) sts.

right front

With 4½mm needles and C, cast on 45 (47: 49) sts.

K 1 row.

Change to 5mm needles and cont in M only.

Next row (right side) K to end.

Moss st row P1, [k1, p1] to end.

This row forms the moss st.

Cont in moss st until front measures 27 (30: 33)cm from cast-on edge, ending with a right side row.

Shape armhole

Cast off 6 sts at beg of next row. 39 (41: 43) sts.

Cont straight until front measures 35 (39: 43)cm from cast-on edge, ending with a wrong side row.

Shape neck

Next row Cast off 15 (16: 17) sts, moss st to end. 24 (25: 26) sts.

Dec 1 st at neck edge on every row until 19 (20: 21) sts rem.

Work straight until front matches Back to shoulder, ending at side edge.

Shape shoulder

Cast off 10 (10: 11) sts at beg of next row.

Work 1 row.

Cast off rem 9 (10: 10) sts.

Place markers for 3 pairs of buttons; the first pair 15 (17: 19)cm from cast-on edge, the third pair 10 (11: 12)cm from neck edge and the remaining pair spaced halfway between.

left front

With 4½mm needles and C, cast on 45 (47: 49) sts.

K 1 row.

Change to 5mm needles and cont in M only.

Next row (right side) K to end.

Moss st row P1, [k1, p1] to end.

This row forms the moss st.

Work as given for Right Front reversing all shapings and working buttonholes to match markers as follows:

Buttonhole row (right side) Moss st 25 (26: 27), work 2 tog, yrn, moss st 14 (15: 16), yrn, p2tog, k1, p1.

collar

Join shoulder seams.
With wrong side facing, 4¹/₂mm needles and M, miss the first 12 (13: 14) cast-off sts of left front neck then pick up and k3 sts from rem cast-off sts, 13 (14: 15) sts up left side of front neck, 21 (23: 25) sts across back neck, 13 (14: 15) sts down right side of right front neck, then 3 sts from the first 3 right front neck cast-off sts. 53 (57: 61) sts.
Next row (right side) K1, [p1, k1] to end.
This row forms the moss st and is repeated.
Next 2 rows Patt to last 14 sts, turn.
Next 2 rows Patt to last 11 sts, turn.
Next 2 rows Patt to last 8 sts, turn.
Next 2 rows Patt to last 5 sts, turn.
Next row Patt to end.
Cont in patt and work a further 6 (6: 7)cm across all sts, ending with a wrong side row.
Break off M.
With right side of collar facing, 4¹/₂mm double-pointed needle and C, pick up and k17 (17: 19) sts along row ends of collar, k across 53 (57: 61) sts on needle, then with a second 4¹/₂mm double-pointed needle, pick up and k17 (17: 19) sts along row ends of collar. 87 (91: 99) sts.
K 1 row. Cast off.

sleeves

With 4¹/₂mm needles and C, cast on 31 (33: 35) sts.
K 1 row.
Change to 5mm needles and cont in M only.
Next row (right side) K to end.
Moss st row P1, * k1, p1; rep from * to end.
This row forms the moss st and is repeated.
Work a further 11 (13: 15) rows and place markers at each end of last row.
Change to 4¹/₂mm needles.
Work a further 12 (14: 16) rows.
Change to 5mm needles.
Inc and work into moss st one st at each end of the next row and every foll 6th row until there are 47 (51: 57) sts.
Cont straight until sleeve measures 24 (27: 30)cm from markers, ending with a wrong side row.
Place a marker at each end of last row.
Work a further 10 rows. Cast off.

right front edging

Mark a point 10 (11: 12)cm down from neck edge.
With wrong side facing, using a 4¹/₂mm double-pointed needle and C, pick up and k12 (13: 14) sts along cast-off edge of neck, then with a second double-pointed needle, pick up and k23 (25: 28) sts down front edge to marker. Break off yarn.
With right side of front facing, 4¹/₂mm needle and C, pick up and k58 (63: 68) sts up right front to marker, break off yarn, slip 23 (25: 28) sts from second double-pointed needle onto same needle.
With wrong side of front (right side of collar) facing, return to first double-pointed needle, p35 (38: 42), k58 (63: 68).
Cast-off row Cast off 58 (63: 68) sts knitwise, then 35 (38: 42) sts purlwise.

left front edging

Mark a point 10 (11: 12)cm from neck edge.

With wrong side facing, a 4¹/₂mm double-pointed needle and C, pick up and k23 (25: 28) sts up front edge from marker to neck edge, then with a second double-pointed needle, pick up and k12 (13: 14) sts along cast-off edge of neck.

Break off yarn.

With right side of front facing, 4¹/₂mm needle and C, pick up and k58 (63: 68) sts down left front.

Next row K58 (63: 68), p35 (38: 42).

Cast-off row Cast off 35 (38: 42) sts purlwise, then 58 (63: 68) sts knitwise.

to make up

With row ends of sleeve above markers sewn to sts cast off at underarm, sew sleeves into armholes, easing to fit. Join side and sleeve seams, reversing seam on cuff. Join row ends of front edging to collar edging. Sew on buttons.

time out

measurements
To fit ages 2–3 (3–4: 4–5) years
actual measurements
Chest 63 (67: 71)cm
Length to centre back neck 30 (33: 36)cm
Sleeve length 22 (25: 28)cm

materials
5 (6: 6) x 50g balls Debbie Bliss Baby Cashmerino in red (M)
1 (1: 1) x 50g ball Debbie Bliss Baby Cashmerino in grey (C)
Pair each $2^3/_4$mm and $3^1/_4$mm knitting needles
$2^3/_4$mm circular knitting needle
4 small buttons

tension
25 sts and 34 rows to 10cm square over st st using $3^1/_4$mm needles.

classic cardigan

back

With 2³/₄mm needles and C, cast on 82 (86: 94) sts.
1st rib row K2, [p2, k2] to end.
2nd rib row P2, [k2, p2] to end.
Change to M.
Next row K to end.
Work a further 5 rows rib and inc 2 sts across last row on 2nd size only. 82 (88: 94) sts.
Change to 3¹/₄mm needles.
Beg with a k row, work in st st until back measures 17 (19: 21)cm from cast-on edge, ending with a p row.
Shape raglans
Cast off 4 sts at beg of next 2 rows. 74 (80: 86) sts.
Next row K2, skpo, k to last 4 sts, k2tog, k2.
Next row P to end.
Rep the last 2 rows until 30 (32: 34) sts rem, ending with a p row. Cast off.

left front

With 2³/₄mm needles and C, cast on 39 (39: 43) sts.
1st rib row K2, [p2, k2] to last 5 sts, p2, k3.
2nd rib row P3, [k2, p2] to end.
** Change to M.
Next row K to end.
Work a further 5 rows rib and inc 2 sts across last row on 2nd size only. 39 (41: 43) sts.
Change to 3¹/₄mm needles.
Beg with a k row, work in st st until left front measures 17 (19: 21)cm from cast-on edge, ending with a p row.**
Shape raglan
Next row (right side) Cast off 4 sts, k to last 4 sts, k2tog, k2. 34 (36: 38) sts.
Next row P to end.
Next row K2, skpo, k to end.
Next row P to end.
Next row K2, skpo, k to last 4 sts, k2tog, k2.
Next row P to end.
Rep the last 4 rows 9 times more. 4 (6: 8) sts
Next row K2, skpo, k to end.
Next row P to end. 3 (5: 7) sts.
2nd and 3rd sizes only
Rep the last 2 rows -(2: 4) times more. 3 sts.
All sizes
Next row K1, skpo.
Next row P to end. Cast off.

right front

With 2³/₄mm needles and C, cast on 39 (39: 43) sts.
1st rib row K3, [p2, k2] to end.
2nd rib row P2, [k2, p2] to last 5 sts, k2, p3.
Work as Left Front from ** to **.
Shape raglan
Next row (right side) K2, skpo, k to end.

Next row Cast off 4 sts, p to end. 34 (36: 38) sts.
Next row K to last 4 sts, k2tog, k2.
Next row P to end.
Next row K2, skpo, k to last 4 sts, k2tog, k2.
Next row P to end.
Rep the last 4 rows 9 times more. 4 (6: 8) sts
Next row K to last 4 sts, k2tog, k2.
Next row P to end. 3 (5: 7) sts.
2nd and 3rd sizes only
Rep the last 2 rows -(2: 4) times more. 3 sts.
All sizes
Next row K2tog, k1.
Next row P to end. Cast off.

sleeves

With 2³/₄mm needles and C, cast on 42 (46: 50) sts.
1st rib row K2, [p2, k2] to end.
2nd rib row P2, [k2, p2] to end.
Change to M.
Next row K to end.
Work a further 5 rows rib.
Change to 3¹/₄mm needles.
Beg with a k row, work in st st.
Work 4 rows.
Inc row K3, m1, k to last 3 sts, m1, k3.
Work 5 rows.
Rep the last 6 rows until there are 62 (70: 78) sts.
Cont straight until sleeve measures 22 (25: 28)cm from cast-on edge, ending with a p row.
Shape raglans
Cast off 4 sts at beg of next 2 rows. 54 (62: 70) sts.
Next row K2, skpo, k to last 4 sts, k2tog, k2.
Next row P to end.
Rep the last 2 rows until 10 (14: 18) sts rem, ending with a p row. Cast off.

front and neck band

Join raglan seams.
With right side facing, 2³/₄mm circular needle and C, pick up and k43 (48: 53) up right front edge to beg of neck shaping, 34 (36: 38) sts along right front neck edge, 8 (12: 16) sts from top of right sleeve, 28 (30: 32) sts from back neck, 8 (12: 16) sts from top of left sleeve, pick up and k34 (36: 38) sts down left front neck edge to beg of neck shaping, 43 (48: 53) down left front edge. 198 (222: 246) sts.
1st rib row P2, [k2, p2] to end.
2nd rib row K2, [p2, k2] to end.
Buttonhole row (wrong side) Rib 157 (175: 193), [rib 2tog, yrn, rib 10 (12: 14)] 3 times, k2tog, yf, rib 3.
Rib 2 more rows. Cast off in rib.

to make up

Join side and sleeve seams. Join underarm seam. Sew on buttons.

measurements

To fit ages 2–3 (3–4: 4–5) years

actual measurements

Chest 61 (66: 71)cm

Length to shoulder 30 (33: 36)cm

materials

4 (4: 5) x 50g balls Debbie Bliss Baby Cashmerino in grey (M)

1 (1: 1) x 50g ball Debbie Bliss Baby Cashmerino in red (C)

Pair each $2^3/_4$mm and $3^1/_4$mm knitting needles

tension

25 sts and 34 rows to 10cm square over st st using $3^1/_4$mm needles.

abbreviations

See page 23.

v neck slipover

back

With $2^3/_4$mm needles and C, cast on 78 (82: 90) sts.

1st rib row K2, [p2, k2] to end.

2nd rib row P2, [k2, p2] to end.

Change to M.

Next row K to end.

Work a further 5 rows in rib and inc 2 sts evenly across last row on 2nd size only. 78 (84: 90) sts.

Change to $3^1/_4$mm needles.

Beg with a k row, work in st st until back measures 17 (19: 21)cm from cast-on edge, ending with a p row.

Shape armholes

Cast off 6 sts at beg of next 2 rows. 66 (72: 78) sts. **

Next row K2, skpo, k to last 2 sts, k2tog, k2.

Next row P to end.

Rep the last 2 rows 5 times more. 54 (60: 66) sts.

Cont in st st until back measures 30 (33: 36)cm from cast-on edge, ending with a p row.

Shape shoulders

Cast off 15 (16: 17) sts at beg of next 2 rows.

Leave rem 24 (28: 32) sts on a spare needle.

front

Work as given for Back to **.

Shape neck

Next row (right side) K2, skpo, k24 (27: 30), k2tog, k2, turn and work on these sts for first side of neck.

Next row P to end.

Next row K2, skpo, k to last 4 sts, k2tog, k2.

Rep the last 2 rows 4 times more. 20 (23: 26) sts.

Keeping armhole edge straight, cont to dec at neck edge on every foll 4th row until 15 (16: 17) sts rem.

Work straight until front measures same as Back to shoulder, ending with a p row.

Cast off.

With right side facing, slip centre 2 sts onto a safety pin, join on yarn to rem sts.

Next row K2, skpo, k24 (27: 30), k2tog, k2.

Next row P to end.

Next row K2, skpo, k to last 4 sts, k2tog, k2.

Rep the last 2 rows 4 times more. 20 (23: 26) sts.

Keeping armhole edge straight, cont to dec at neck edge on every foll 4th row until 15 (16: 17) sts rem.

Work straight until front measures same as Back to shoulder, ending with a p row.

Cast off.

neckband

Join right shoulder seam.

With right side facing, 2³/₄mm needles and M, pick up and k34 (38: 42) sts evenly down left side of front neck, k2 from safety pin, pick up and k34 (38: 42) sts evenly up right side of front neck, k24 (28: 32) sts from back neck holder. 94 (106: 118) sts.

1st row K2, [p2, k2] to end.

2nd row Rib 33 (37: 41), k2tog, skpo, rib to end.

3rd row Rib to end.

4th row Rib 32 (36: 40), k2tog, skpo, rib to end.

5th row Rib to end.

Change to C.

6th row K31 (35: 39), k2tog, skpo, k to end

7th row Rib to end.

Cast off in rib, and dec on this row as before.

armbands

Join left shoulder and neckband seam.

With right side facing, 2³/₄mm needles and M, pick up and k86 (94: 102) sts along armhole edge.

Work 5 rows in rib as given for Back.

Change to C.

6th row K to end.

7th row Rib to end.

Cast off in rib.

to make up

Join side and armband seams.

measurements

To fit ages 2–3 (3–4: 4–5) years
actual measurements
Chest 78 (82: 86)cm
Length to shoulder 50 (54: 58)cm
Sleeve length with cuff turned back 24 (27: 30)cm

materials

15 (16: 17) x 50g balls Debbie Bliss Rialto Aran in pale blue
Pair each 4½mm and 5mm knitting needles
40 (45: 50)cm open-ended zip

tension

19 sts and 36 rows to 10cm square over moss st using 5mm needles.

abbreviations

y2rn = yarn round needle twice to make 2 sts.
Also see page 23.

anorak

back

Right side
With 4½mm needles, cast on 40 (42: 44) sts.
K 3 rows.
Change to 5mm needles.
Next row [P1, k1] to last 4 sts, k4.
Next row (wrong side) K4, [k1, p1] 2 (3: 4) times, turn.
Next row [P1, k1] 2 (3: 4) times, k4.
Next row K4, [k1, p1] 4 (5: 6) times, turn.
Next row [P1, k1] 4 (5: 6) times, k4.
Next row K4, [k1, p1] 6 (7: 8) times, turn.
Next row [P1, k1] 6 (7: 8) times, k4.
Next row K4, [k1, p1] 8 (9: 10) times, turn.
Next row [P1, k1] 8 (9: 10) times, k4.
Cont in this way working an extra 4 sts on every alt row until all the sts have been taken into moss st with 5 sts in garter st, ending with a right side row.
Place a marker at beg of last row.
Next row (wrong side) K5, moss st to end.
Next row Moss st to last 5 sts, k5.
Rep the last 2 rows until side seam (moss st edge) measures 23 (26: 29)cm from cast-on edge, ending with a right side row.

Break yarn and leave these sts on a holder.

Mark the position on the garter st edging for 4 buttons, the first level with marker, the fourth 4cm below top edge with two spaced evenly between.

Left side

With 4½mm needles, cast on 40 (42: 44) sts.

K 3 rows.

Change to 5mm needles.

Next row (right side) K4, [k1, p1] 2 (3: 4) times, turn.

Next row [P1, k1] 2 (3: 4) times, k4.

Next row K4, [k1, p1] 4 (5: 6) times, turn,

Next row [P1, k1] 4 (5: 6) times, k4.

Next row K4, [k1, p1] 6 (7: 8) times, turn.

Next row [P1, k1] 6 (7: 8) times, k4.

Next row K4, [k1, p1] 8 (9: 10) times, turn.

Next row [P1, k1] 8 (9: 10) times, k4.

Cont in this way working an extra 4 sts on every alt row until all the sts have been taken into moss st with 5 sts in garter st, ending with a wrong side row.

Buttonhole row K1, k2tog, y2rn, skpo, moss st to end.

Cont in moss st and garter st patt, working buttonholes to match markers, until side seam (moss st edge) measures 23 (26: 29)cm from cast-on edge, ending with a right side row.

Joining row (wrong side) Moss st 35 (37: 39), place right back on top of left back, [k next st of left back tog with next st of right back] 5 times, moss st to end. 75 (79: 83) sts

Cord channel

Beg with a k row, work 4 rows in st st.

Do not break yarn, leave these sts on a spare needle.

Channel back

With wrong side facing, working down through sts, miss first st, then pick up and k 1 st from each st along first k row, miss last st, turn. (This will be wrong side of work facing but 'right' side of st st.)

Beg with a k row, work 4 rows st st.

Break yarn, slip stitches from one needle to another.

Return to main part.

Next row K1, [k next st of main part tog with next st of channel back] 73 (77: 81) times, k1. 75 (79: 83) sts.

Cont in moss st until back measures 37 (40: 43)cm from cast-on edge, ending with a wrong side row.

Shape armholes

Cast off 6 sts at beg of next 2 rows. 63 (67: 71) sts.

Cont straight until back measures 50 (54: 58)cm from cast-on edge, ending with a wrong side row.

Shape shoulders

Cast off 10 (10: 11) sts at beg of next 2 rows and 10 (11: 11) sts at beg of foll 2 rows.

Cast off rem 23 (25: 27) sts.

left front

With 4½mm needles, cast on 38 (40: 42) sts.

K 3 rows.

Change to 5mm needles.

1st row (right side) [K1, p1] to last 2 sts, k2.

2nd row K2, [p1, k1] to end.

These 2 rows form moss st with garter st front edging.

Cont in moss st until front measures 23 (26: 29)cm from cast-on edge, ending with a wrong side row.

Cord channel

Next row K28 (30: 32), turn and leave rem 10 sts on a spare needle.

Next row K2, p to end.

Next row K to end.

Next row K2, p to end.

Do not break yarn, leave these sts on a holder.

With wrong side facing, working down through sts, miss first st, then pick up and k 1 st from each st along first k row, 22 (29: 31) times, then patt across 10 sts on holder. (This will be wrong side of work facing but 'right' side of st st.)

Next row Patt 10 sts, k to end.

Next row P to last 10 sts, patt to end.

Next row Patt 10 sts, k to end.

Break yarn.

Return to main part.

Next row K1, [k next st of main part tog with next st of channel back] 22 (29: 31) times, patt to end. 38 (40: 42) sts.

Cont in moss st with garter st edging until front measures 37 (40: 43)cm from cast-on edge, ending with a wrong side row.

Shape armhole

Cast off 6 sts at beg of next row. 32 (34: 36) sts.

Cont straight until front measures 45 (49: 53)cm from cast-on edge, ending with a wrong side row.

Shape neck

Next row Patt to last 6 (7: 8) sts, turn and work on these 26 (27: 28) sts only, leave rem 6 (7: 8) sts on a holder for hood.

Dec 1 st at neck edge on next 6 rows. 20 (21: 22) sts.

Work straight until front matches Back to shoulder, ending at side edge.

Shape shoulder

Cast off 10 (10: 11) sts at beg of next row.

Work 1 row. Cast off rem 10 (11: 11) sts.

right front

With 4 1/2 mm needles, cast on 38 (40: 42) sts.

K 3 rows.

Change to 5mm needles.

1st row (right side) K2, [p1, k1] to end.

2nd row [K1, p1] to last 2 sts, k2.

These 2 rows form moss st with garter st front edging.

Cont in moss st until front measures 23 (26: 29)cm from cast-on edge, ending with a wrong side row.

Cord Channel

Next row Patt 10, leave these sts on a holder, k28 (30: 32).

Next row P to last 2 sts, k2.

Next row K to end.

Next row P to last 2 sts, k2.
Break off yarn, leave these sts on a spare needle.
Slip the 10 sts from holder onto a 5mm needle, then with wrong side facing, working down through sts, pick up and k 1 st from each st along first k row, 22 (29: 31) times, k last st. (This will be wrong side of work facing but 'right' side of st st.)
Next row K to last 10 sts, patt to end.
Next row Patt 10 sts, p to end.
Next row K to last 10 sts, patt to end.
Return to main part.
Next row Patt 10, [k next st of main part tog with next st of back] 22 (29: 31) times, k1. 38 (40: 42) sts.
Cont in moss st with garter st edging until front measures 37 (40: 43)cm from cast-on edge, ending with a right side row.
Shape armhole
Cast off 6 sts at beg of next row. 32 (34: 36) sts.
Cont straight until front measures 45 (49: 53)cm from cast-on edge, ending with a wrong side row.
Shape neck
Next row P6 (7: 8) sts and slip these sts onto a holder, patt to end. 26 (27: 28) sts.
Dec 1 st at neck edge on next 6 rows. 20 (21: 22) sts.
Work straight until front matches Back to shoulder, ending at side edge.
Shape shoulder
Cast off 10 (10: 11) sts at beg of next row.
Work 1 row. Cast off rem 10 (11: 11) sts.

sleeves

With 4¹/₂mm needles, cast on 31 (33: 35) sts.
Change to 5mm needles.
Moss st row (wrong side) P1, [k1, p1] to end.
This row forms the moss st and is repeated.
Work a further 12 (14: 16) rows.

Inc and work into moss st one st at each end of the next row and every foll 8th row until there are 47 (51: 57) sts.

Cont straight until sleeve measures 27 (30: 33)cm from cast-on edge, ending with a wrong side row.

Place markers at each end of last row.

Work a further 10 rows.

Cast off.

hood

Join shoulder seams.

With wrong side facing and 4^1/$_2$mm needles, slip 6 (7: 8) sts from right front holder onto a needle, pick up and k12 sts up right side of front neck, cast on 35 (39: 43) sts, pick up and k12 sts down left side of front neck, then patt across 6 (7: 8) sts on left front holder. 71 (77: 83) sts.

Cont in moss st with garter st edging.

Work 3 rows.

Next row K2, m1, moss st to last 2 sts, m1, k2.

Work 7 rows.

Rep the last 8 rows 7 (8: 9) times more and the inc row again. 89 (97: 105) sts.

Work 1 row.

Next row Patt 43 (47: 51), work 3 tog, patt to end.

Next row Patt to end.

Next row Patt 42 (46: 50), work 3 tog, patt to end.

Next row Patt to end.

Next row Patt 41 (45: 49), work 3 tog, patt to end.

Next row Patt to end.

Next row Patt 40 (44: 48), work 3 tog, patt to end.

Next row Patt to end.

Cast off.

left lower pocket

** With 5mm needles, cast on 19 (21: 23) sts.
Moss st row K1, [p1, k1] to end.
This row forms moss st and is repeated. **
Cont in moss st until pocket measures 8 (9: 10)cm from cast-on edge, ending with a right side row.
Shape top
Next 2 rows Moss st to last 4 sts, turn, moss st to end.
Next 2 rows Moss st to last 8 sts, turn, moss st to end.
Next 2 rows Moss st to last 12 sts, turn, moss st to end.
Next 2 rows Moss st to last 16 sts, turn, moss st to end.
Next row Moss st to end.
Change to 4 1/2 mm needles.
K 2 rows.
Buttonhole row K8 (9: 10), k2tog, y2rn, skpo, k to end.
K 2 rows.
Cast off.

right lower pocket

Work as Left Lower Pocket from ** to **.
Cont in moss st until pocket measures 8 (9: 10)cm from cast-on edge, ending with a wrong side row.
Shape top
Next 2 rows Moss st to last 4 sts, turn, moss st to end.
Next 2 rows Moss st to last 8 sts, turn, moss st to end.
Next 2 rows Moss st to last 12 sts, turn, moss st to end.
Next 2 rows Moss st to last 16 sts, turn, moss st to end.
Change to 4 1/2 mm needles.
K 2 rows.
Buttonhole row K7 (8: 9), k2tog, y2rn, skpo, k to end.
K 2 rows. Cast off.

mock pocket flap (make 2)

With 5mm needles, cast on 19 (21: 23) sts.
Patt row K2, [p1, k1] to last 3 sts, p1, k2.
Rep this row 11 times more.
K 2 rows.
Buttonhole row K8 (9: 10), k2tog, y2rn, skpo, k to end.
K 2 rows. Cast off.

cord

With 4 1/2 mm needles, cast on 4 sts.
Beg with a k row, work in st st until tie measures 150cm, ending with a p row.
Next row [K2tog] twice, thread yarn through remaining 2 sts and fasten off.

to make up

Sew sleeves into armholes with row ends above markers sewn to sts cast off at underarm. Join side and sleeve seams reversing seam on last 3cm for turn back. Sew cast-on edge of hood to sts cast off at back neck, easing to fit. Sew on pockets and mock pocket flaps. Sew on buttons. Thread cord through channel to tie at centre front. Hand-sew zip in place, beg at neck edge.

hoodie

measurements

To fit ages 2–3 (3–4: 4–5) years

actual measurements

Chest 73 (80: 88)cm

Length to shoulder 35 (40: 45)cm

Sleeve length with cuff turned back 22 (25: 28)cm

materials

8 (9: 10) x 50g balls Debbie Bliss Rialto Aran in green

Pair each 4$\frac{1}{2}$mm and 5mm knitting needles

Cable needle

tension

18 sts and 24 rows to 10cm square over st st using 5mm needles.

abbreviations

C4B = slip next 2 sts onto a cable needle and hold at back of work, k2, then k2 from cable needle.

C4F = slip next 2 sts onto a cable needle and hold at front of work, k2, then k2 from cable needle.

m1pw = make 1 st by picking up and purling into back of loop lying between st just worked and next st.

Also see page 23.

back

With 4 1/2 mm needles, cast on 66 (74: 82) sts.
1st row K2, [p2, k2] to end.
2nd row P2, [k2, p2] to end.
Rep the last 2 rows 5 times more, inc 2 sts across last row on 1st size only. 68 (74: 82) sts.
Change to 5mm needles.
Beg with a k row, work in st st until back measures 21 (25: 29)cm from cast-on edge, ending with a p row.
Shape armholes
Next row Cast off 7 (6: 5) sts, k to end.
Next row Cast off 7 (6: 5) sts, with 1 st on needle after cast off, p next 5 (9: 9) sts, [m1pw, p2, m1pw, p8] 4 (4: 5) times, m1pw, p2, m1pw, p6 (10: 10). 64 (72: 84) sts.
Work in yoke patt as follows:
1st row (right side) P1, [k2, p2] 1 (2: 2) times, [k2, C4F, p2, k2, p2] 4 (4: 5) times, k2, C4F, [p2, k2] 1 (2: 2) times, p1.
2nd row K1, [p2, k2] 1 (2: 2) times, p6, [k2, p2, k2, p6] 4 (4: 5) times, [k2, p2] 1 (2: 2) times, k1.
3rd row P1, [k2, p2] 1 (2: 2) times, [C4B, k2, p2, k2, p2] 4 (4: 5) times, C4B, k2, [p2, k2] 1 (2: 2) times, p1.
4th row K1, [p2, k2] 1 (2: 2) times, p6, [k2, p2, k2, p6] 4 (4: 5) times, [k2, p2] 1 (2: 2) times, k1.
These 4 rows form the patt and are repeated. **
Cont in patt until back measures 33 (38: 43)cm from cast-on edge, ending with a wrong side row.
Shape back neck
Next row Patt 21 (24: 29), turn and work on these sts only for first side of neck shaping.
Next row Patt 2 tog, patt to end.
Next row Patt to last 2 sts, patt 2 tog.
Next row Patt to end. 19 (22: 27) sts.
Cast off.
With right side facing, slip centre 22 (24: 26) sts onto a holder, rejoin yarn to rem sts, patt to end.
Complete to match first side, reversing shaping.

front

Work as given for Back to **.
Cont in patt until front measures 30 (34: 38)cm from cast-on edge, ending with a wrong side row.
Shape front neck
Next row Patt 24 (27: 32), turn and work on these sts for first side of neck shaping.
Dec 1 st at neck on every foll alt row until 19 (22: 27) sts rem.
Work straight until front measures same as Back to shoulder, ending at armhole edge.
Cast off.
With right side facing, slip centre 16 (18: 20) sts onto a holder, rejoin yarn to rem sts, patt to end.
Complete to match first side, reversing shaping.

sleeves

With 4 1/2 mm needles, cast on 34 (38: 42) sts.
1st row K2, [p2, k2] to end.
2nd row P2, [k2, p2] to end.
Rep the last 2 rows 5 times more.
Change to 5mm needles
Beg with a k row, work in st st.
Work 2 rows.

Inc row K3, m1, k to last 3 sts, m1, k3.

Work 3 rows.

Rep the last 4 rows 7 (8: 9) times more and the inc row again. 52 (58: 64) sts.

Next row P5 (8: 6) sts, [m1pw, p2, m1pw, p8] 4 (4: 5) times, m1pw, p2, m1pw, p5 (8: 6). 62 (68: 76) sts.

Cont in patt as follows:

1st row K2 (5: 3), p2, [k2, C4F, p2, k2, p2] 4 (4: 5) times, k2, C4F, p2, k2 (5: 3).

2nd row P2 (5: 3), k2, p6, [k2, p2, k2, p6] 4 (4: 5) times, k2, p2 (5: 3).

3rd row K2 (5: 3), p2, [C4B, k2, p2, k2, p2] 4 (4: 5) times, C4B, k2, p2, k2 (5: 3).

4th row P2 (5: 3), k2, p6, [k2, p2, k2, p6] 4 (4: 5) times, k2, p2 (5: 3).

These 4 rows form the patt and are repeated.

Cont in patt until sleeve measures 22 (25: 28)cm from cast-on edge, ending with a wrong side row.

Place markers at each end of last row.

Work a further 10 rows.

Cast off.

neckband

Join right shoulder seam.
With right side facing and 4¹/₂mm needles, pick up and k11 sts down left front neck, k across 16 (18: 20) sts from front neck, pick up and k11 sts up right front neck, 5 sts down right back neck, k across 22 (24: 26) sts from back neck, then pick up and k5 sts up left back neck. 70 (74: 78) sts.
1st row P2, [k2, p2] to end.
2nd row K2, [p2, k2] to end.
Rep the last 2 rows once more and the 1st row again.
Cast off in rib.

hood

With 5mm needles, cast on 86 (94: 102) sts.
Beg with a k row, work in st st until hood measures 20 (23: 26)cm from cast-on edge, ending with a p row.
Change to 4¹/₂mm needles.
1st row K2, [p2, k2] to end.
2nd row P2, [k2, p2] to end.
Rep the last 2 rows twice more.
Cast off in rib.

pocket

With 4¹/₂mm needles, cast on 24 (28: 30) sts.
1st row K3, [p2, k2] to last 5 sts, p2, k3.
2nd row P3, [k2, p2] to last 5 sts, k2, p3.
Rep the last 2 rows twice more.
Change to 5mm needles.
Beg with a k row, work in st st until pocket measures 16 (18: 20)cm, ending with a p row.
Change to 4¹/₂mm needles.
1st row K3, [p2, k2] to last 5 sts, p2, k3.
2nd row P3, [k2, p2] to last 5 sts, k2, p3.
Rep the last 2 rows twice more.
Cast off.

to make up

Join left shoulder and neckband seam. Sew sleeves into armholes with row ends above markers are sewn to sts cast off at underarm. Join side and sleeve seams. Sew pocket to front. Fold hood in half and join cast-on edges to form back seam. Sew hood in place inside neckband.

measurements
Length approximately 21cm
Height approximately 9cm

materials
1 x 50g ball of Debbie Bliss Rialto DK in each of red (A), pink (B), lime (C), grey (D) and duck egg (E)
OR approximately 18m in each of 5 shades of Debbie Bliss Rialto DK
Pair 3³/₄mm knitting needles
20 x 23cm piece of lining fabric
20cm zip fastener
Sewing thread and needle

tension
24 sts and 48 rows to 10cm square over garter st using 3³/₄mm needles.

abbreviations
See page 23.

pencil case

to make

With 3³/₄mm needles and A, cast on 42 sts.
K 1 row.
Cont in garter st (k every row), change colour and work 2-row stripes of each colour randomly until work measures 21cm, ending with the 1st row of a 2-row stripe in A.
Cast off knitwise in A.

to make up

Fold knitting in half lengthways and join folded cast-on and cast-off edges, so leaving row-end edges open. Pin, tack and hand stitch zip in place, tucking all yarn ends in behind zip tape and taking care to match stripes.
Fold lining fabric in half lengthways and taking 1cm seams, join folded short ends. Press 1cm around open edges onto wrong side. Insert lining into pencil case and hand stitch lining to zip tape.
Cut a few lengths of assorted colour yarns and thread through zip pull to assist opening and closing of pencil case.

measurements

Size approximately 20 x 24 x 5cm

materials

5 x 50g balls Debbie Bliss Rialto DK in navy (M)
1 x 50g ball Debbie Bliss Rialto DK in red (C)
Pair 4 1/2 mm knitting needles
0.5m of lining fabric
1m of 4cm wide red cotton webbing
2 kilt straps

tension

18.5 sts and 27 rows to 10cm square over st st using 4 1/2 mm needles and two lengths
of yarn together.

notes

The satchel is worked in one piece from the lower edge of the front flap.
Double yarn is used throughout.

satchel

to make

Front flap

With 4 1/2 mm needles and two balls of M held and used together, cast on 41 sts.
Moss st row K1, [p1, k1] to end.
Rep this row 3 times more.
Next row (right side) [K1, p1] twice, k33, [p1, k1] twice.
Next row [K1, p1] twice, p33, [p1, k1] twice.
Rep the last 2 rows until work measures 12cm from cast-on edge, ending with a wrong side row.
Moss st 4 rows.
Next row [K1, p1] twice, k33, [p1, k1] twice.
Ridge row [K1, p1] twice, k33, [p1, k1] twice.

Back

Next row [K1, p1] twice, k33, [p1, k1] twice.
Moss st 4 rows.
** **Next row** (wrong side) [K1, p1] twice, p33, [p1, k1] twice.
Next row [K1, p1] twice, k33, [p1, k1] twice.
Rep the last 2 rows for 16cm from **, ending with a wrong side row.
Moss st 4 rows.
Next row [K1, p1] twice, k33, [p1, k1] twice.
Ridge row (wrong side) [K1, p1] twice, k33, [p1, k1] twice.

Base
Next row [K1, p1] twice, k33, [p1, k1] twice.
Moss st 4 rows.
Next row (wrong side) [K1, p1] twice, p33, [p1, k1] twice.
Next row [K1, p1] twice, k33, [p1, k1] twice.
Rep the last 2 rows once more and the first of these 2 rows again.
Moss st 4 rows.
Next row [K1, p1] twice, k33, [p1, k1] twice.
Ridge row (wrong side) [K1, p1] twice, k33, [p1, k1] twice.
Front
Next row [K1, p1] twice, k33, [p1, k1] twice.
Moss st 4 rows.
Next row (wrong side) [K1, p1] twice, p33, [p1, k1] twice.
Next row [K1, p1] twice, k33, [p1, k1] twice.
Rep the last 2 rows 4 times more and the first of these 2 rows again.
Next row (right side) With M, [k1, p1] twice, k6, with C, k21, with M, k6, [p1, k1] twice.
Next row With M, [k1, p1] twice, p6, with C, p21, with M, p6, [p1, k1] twice.
Rep the last 2 rows 10 times more.
Next row With M, [k1, p1] twice, p33, [p1, k1] twice.
Cont in M only and work 4 rows in moss st.
Cast off in moss st.

gusset strap

With 4½mm needles and two lengths of M, cast on 9 sts.
Moss st row K1, [p1, k1] to end.
Rep this row until gusset strap measures approximately 1m from cast-on edge.
Cast off in moss st.

front pocket

With 4½mm needles and two lengths of M, cast on 29 sts.
Moss st row K1, [p1, k1] to end.
Rep the last row 3 times more.
1st row [K1, p1] twice, k21, [p1, k1] twice.
2nd row {K1, p1] twice, p21, [p1, k1] to end.
Rep these 2 rows 8 times more.
Shape gusset
Next 2 rows Cast off 4 sts, moss st to end. 21 sts.
Work 5 rows in moss st for pocket base.
Cast off in moss st.

to make up

Sew short cast-off edges of pocket to moss st row ends of pocket base. Sew side and base edges of pocket to contrast colour area on satchel front. Sew webbing to gusset strip to prevent over-stretching. Sew cast-on and cast-off edges of gusset strip to row ends of satchel base between ridge rows. Sew edges of satchel front to gusset strip. Sew edges of satchel back to gusset strip from base to end of st st section. Hand stitch kilt straps to front of satchel, either side of pocket.

lining

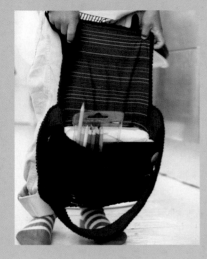

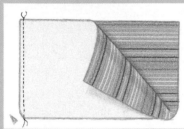

fig 1

fig 2

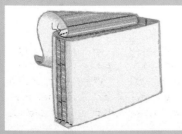

fig 3

For the main bag, cut a piece of lining fabric 31 x 36cm. Fold in half so making a rectangle 31 x 18cm and sew the side seams, taking a 1.5cm seam allowance. Clip corners at the fold and press seams open. Refold and stitch 5cm across the points so forming the base, trim excess fabric.

For the satchel flap lining, cut a second piece of fabric, 21.5 x 25cm. With right sides together and taking a 1.5cm seam allowance, stitch one longer side centrally to the top edge of the main bag lining leaving 1.5cm at each end of seam unstitched. Press seam open and continue to press 1.5cm around top of main bag lining onto wrong side, then press 1.5cm around the three unstitched edges of flap lining onto wrong side. Insert lining into satchel and slip stitch in place around pressed edges.

scarf coat

measurements

To fit ages 2–3 (3–4: 4–5) years

actual measurements

Chest 76 (80: 85)cm

Length to shoulder 48 (52: 56)cm

Sleeve length with cuff turned back 24 (27: 30)cm

materials

10 (12: 14) x 50g balls Debbie Bliss Rialto Aran in berry (M)

1 (1: 1) x 50g ball Debbie Bliss Rialto Aran in pale blue (C)

Pair each 4¹/₂mm and 5mm knitting needles

5mm circular knitting needle

2 large buttons

tension

18 sts and 30 rows to 10cm square over moss st using 5mm needles.

abbreviations

y2rn = yarn round needle twice to make 2 sts.

Also see page 23.

back

With 4¹/₂mm needles and M, cast on 89 (93: 97) sts.

K 3 rows.

Change to 5mm needles.

Moss st row K1, [p1, k1] to end.

Repeating last row to form moss st, work a further 9 (15: 21) rows in moss st.

Dec row (right side) Moss st 6, k3tog, moss st to last 9 sts, k3tog, moss st 6.

Moss st 19 rows.

Rep the last 20 rows 3 times more and the dec row again. 69 (73: 77) sts.

Moss st 7 rows.

Shape armholes

Cast off 4 sts at beg of next 2 rows. 61 (65: 69) sts.

Leave these sts on a spare needle.

left front

With 4¹/₂mm needles and M, cast on 47 (49: 51) sts.

K 3 rows.

Change to 5mm needles.

Next row P1, [k1, p1] to last 6 sts, k6.

Next row K6, p1, [k1, p1] to end.

These 2 rows form the moss st with garter st edging.

Work a further 8 (14: 20) rows.

Dec row (right side) Moss st 6, p3tog, moss st to last to last 6 sts, k6.
Patt 19 rows.
Dec row (right side) Moss st 6, p3tog, moss st to last to last 6 sts, k6. 43 (45: 47) sts.
Patt 3 rows.
Pocket opening
Next row Moss st 16 (18: 20), turn and work on these sts only, leave rem 27 sts on a holder.
Work 15 rows.
Dec row (right side) Moss st 6, p3tog, moss st to end.
Work 14 rows.
Leave these sts on a holder.
With right side facing, rejoin yarn to rem sts, patt to end.
Work a further 30 rows, so ending with a right side row.
Next row Moss st 27, then with wrong side of first side facing, moss st to end. 41 (43: 45) sts.
Work 4 rows.
Dec row (right side) Moss st 6, p3tog, moss st to last to last 6 sts, k6.
Patt 19 rows.
Dec row (right side) Moss st 6, p3tog, moss st to last to last 6 sts, k6. 37 (39: 41) sts.
Patt 7 rows.
Shape armholes
Cast off 4 sts at beg of next row. 33 (35: 37) sts.
Patt 1 row.
Leave these sts on a spare needle.

right front

With 4¹/₂mm needles and M, cast on 47 (49: 51) sts.
K 3 rows.
Change to 5mm needles.
Next row K6, p1, [k1, p1] to end.
Next row P1, [k1, p1] to last 6 sts, k6.
These 2 rows form the moss st with garter st edging.
Work a further 8 (14: 20) rows.
Dec row (right side) K6, moss st to last 9 sts, p3tog, moss st 6.
Patt 19 rows.
Dec row K6, moss st to last 9 sts, p3tog, moss st 6. 43 (45: 47) sts.
Patt 3 rows.
Pocket opening
Next row (right side) K6, moss st 21, turn and work on these sts only, leave rem 16 (18: 20) sts on a holder.
Work 30 rows, so ending with a right side row.
Leave these sts on a holder.
With right side facing, rejoin yarn to rem 16 (18: 20) sts, patt to end.
Work 15 rows.
Dec row Moss st to last 9 sts, p3tog, moss st 6.
Work 14 rows.
Next row Moss st 14 (16: 18) then with wrong side of first side facing, moss st to end. 41 (43: 47) sts.
Work 4 rows.

● ● ● ● ● ● ● ● ● ● ● ◉

Dec row K6, moss st to last 9 sts, p3tog, moss st 6.
Patt 19 rows.
Dec row K6, moss st to last 9 sts, p3tog, moss st 6. 37 (39: 41) sts.
Patt 8 rows.
Shape armhole
Cast off 4 sts at beg of next row. 33 (35: 37) sts.
Leave these sts on a spare needle.

left sleeve

With 4 1/2mm needles and M, cast on 30 (34: 38) sts.
K 3 rows.
Change to 5mm needles.
1st moss st row (right side of cuff, wrong side of sleeve) [P1, k1] to end.
2nd moss st row [K1, p1] to end.
Work a further 11 (13: 15) rows.
Place markers at each end of last row.
Change to 4 1/2mm needles.
Work 12 (14: 16) rows.
Change to 5mm needles.
Inc and work into moss st one st at each end of 3rd (5th: 7th) row and every foll 6th row until there are 50 (54: 58) sts.
Cont straight until sleeve measures 24 (27: 30)cm from markers, ending with a wrong side row.
Shape top
Cast off 4 sts at beg of next 2 rows. 42 (46: 50) sts.
Leave these sts on a spare needle.

right sleeve

Work as given for Left Sleeve, reading k for p and p for k.

yoke

With right side facing and 5mm circular needle, k6, moss st 26 (28: 30) across sts of right front, work last st tog with first st of right sleeve, moss st 40 (44: 48), work last st of sleeve tog with first st of back, moss st 59 (63: 67), work last st of back tog with first st of left sleeve, moss st 40 (44: 48), work last st of sleeve tog with first st of left front, moss st 26 (28: 30), k7. 207 (223: 239) sts.
Patt row K6, moss st to last 6 sts, k6.
Patt 2 rows.
4th row Patt 31 (33: 35), work 3 tog, moss st 38 (42: 46), work 3 tog, moss st 57 (61: 65), work 3 tog, moss st 38 (42: 46), work 3 tog, patt 31 (33: 35). 199 (215: 231) sts.
Patt 3 rows.
8th row Patt 30 (32: 34), work 3 tog, moss st 36 (40: 44), work 3 tog, moss st 55 (59: 63), work 3 tog, moss st 36 (40: 44), work 3 tog, patt 30 (32: 34). 191 (207: 223) sts.
Patt 3 rows.
12th row Patt 29 (31: 33), work 3 tog, moss st 34 (38: 42), work 3 tog, moss st 53 (57: 61), work 3 tog, moss st 34 (38: 42), work 3 tog, patt 29 (31: 33). 183 (199: 215) sts.
Patt 1 row.
Buttonhole row K2, k2tog, y2rn, skpo, patt to end.
Patt 1 row.

Working a buttonhole on the foll 25th (27th: 29th) row, cont in this way to dec 8 sts on next row and 3 foll 4th rows, then on 11 (12: 13) foll right side rows. 63 (71: 79) sts.
Next row (wrong side) Cast off 17 (19: 21) sts, cast on 41 (43: 45), moss st to end, cast on 51 sts. 138 (146: 154) sts.
Work 3cm in moss st, ending with a wrong side row.
Next row Moss st 31, cast off 14 sts, moss st to end.
Next row Moss st to end, casting on 14 sts over those cast off in previous row.
Moss st a further 8cm.
Cast off in moss st.

right pocket lining

With right side facing, 4¹/₂mm needles and C, pick up and k 20 sts along back edge of pocket opening.
Next row P to end.
Next row Cast on 9 (11: 13) sts, k to end.
Work a further 21 (23: 25) rows in st st.
Cast off.

left pocket lining

With right side facing, 4¹/₂mm needles and C, pick up and k 20 sts along back edge of pocket opening.
Next row P to end.
Next row K to end.
Next row Cast on 9 (11: 13) sts, p to end.
Work a further 21 (23: 25) rows in st st. Cast off.

to make up

Join side and sleeve seams, reversing seam below markers. Join underarm seam. Sew on buttons. Slipstitch pocket linings in place.

yarndistributors

143

For stockists of Debbie Bliss
yarns please contact:

UK & WORLDWIDE DISTRIBUTORS
Designer Yarns Ltd
Units 8–10
Newbridge Industrial Estate
Pitt Street, Keighley
W. Yorkshire BD21 4PQ
UK
t: +44 (0) 1535 664222
f: +44 (0) 1535 664333
e: alex@designeryarns.uk.com
w: www.designeryarns.uk.com

USA
Knitting Fever Inc.
315 Bayview Avenue
Amityville
NY 11701
USA
t: +1 516 546 3600
f: +1 516 546 6871
w: www.knittingfever.com

CANADA
Diamond Yarns Ltd
155 Martin Ross Avenue Unit 3
Toronto
Ontario M3J 2L9
Canada
t: +1 416 736 6111
f: +1 416 736 6112
w: www.diamondyarn.com

BELGIUM/HOLLAND
Pavan
Meerlaanstraat 73
9860 Balegem (Oostrezele)
Belgium
t: +32 (0) 9 221 85 94
f: +32 (0) 9 221 56 62
e: pavan@pandora.be

DENMARK
Fancy Knit
Hovedvejen 71
8586 Oerum Djurs
Ramten
Denmark
t: +45 59 46 21 89
f: +45 59 46 8018
e: roenneburg@mail.dk

FINLAND
Duo Design
Kaikukuja 1 c 31
00530 Helsinki
Finland
t: +358 (0) 9 753 1716
e: maria.hellbom@priima.net
w: www.duodesign.fi

FRANCE
Elle Tricote
8 Rue du Coq
La Petite France
67000 Strasbourg
France
t: +33 (0) 388 230313
f: +33 (0) 8823 0169
w: www.elletricote.com

GERMANY/AUSTRIA/
SWITZERLAND/LUXEMBOURG
Designer Yarns (Deutschland) Ltd
Sachsstraße 30
D-50259 Pulheim-Brauweiler
Germany
t: +49 (0) 2234 205453
f: +49 (0) 2234 205456
e: kk@designeryarns.de
w: www.designeryarns.de

ICELAND
Storkurinn ehf
Laugavegi 59
101 Reykjavík
Iceland
t: +354 551 8258
f: +354 562 8252
e: storkurinn@simnet.is

SPAIN
Oyambre Needlework SL
Balmes, 200 At. 4
08006 Barcelona
Spain
t: +34 (0) 93 487 26 72
f: +34 (0) 93 218 66 94
e: info@oyambreonline.com

SWEDEN
Nysta garn och textil
Luntmakargatan 50
S-113 58 Stockholm
Sweden
t: +46 (0) 8 612 0330
e: nina@nysta.se
w: www.nysta.se

AUSTRALIA/NEW ZEALAND
Prestige Yarns Pty Ltd
PO Box 39
Bulli
NSW 2516
Australia
t: +61 (0) 2 4285 6669
e: info@prestigeyarns.com
w: www.prestigeyarns.com

BRAZIL
Quatro Estacoes Com
Las Linhas e Acessorios Ltda
Av. Das Nacoes Unidas
12551-9 Andar
Cep 04578-000 Sao Paulo
Brazil
t: +55 11 3443 7736
e: cristina@4estacoeslas.com.br

MEXICO
Estambres Crochet SA de CV
Aaron Saenz 1891–7
Col. Santa Maria
Monterrey
N.L. 64650
Mexico
t: +52 (81) 8335 3870
e: abremer@redmundial.com.mx

For more information on my
other books and yarns, please
visit www.debbieblissonline.com

acknowledgements

This book would not have been possible without the contribution of the following:

Jane O'Shea, **Lisa Pendreigh** and **Mary Evans** at Quadrille Publishing who have been such an inspirational team to work with.

Julie Mansfield, the stylist, whose input, as always, has been invaluable.

Ulla Nyeman, for the simply beautiful photographs, and her assistants.

Sally Kvalheim, who did such a great job baby grooming.

And, of course, the fantastic kids: **AJ**, **Alfie**, **Angus**, **Carson**, **Elina**, **Erin**, **Femi**, **Iona**, **Jacob**, **LeiLei**, **Litzi**, **Shianne**, **Thomas**, **Tilda**, **Tilly** and **Tirion**.

Rosy Tucker, not only for pattern checking but for her wonderful design and creative contribution.

Penny Hill, for her essential pattern compiling and organising the knitters.

The knitters, for the huge effort they put into creating perfectly knitted garments under deadline pressure: **Cynthia Brent**, **Barbara Clapham**, **Pat Church**, **Pat Clack**, **Jacqui Dunt**, **Shirley Kennet**, **Maisie Lawrence** and **Frances Wallace**.

My fantastic agent, **Heather Jeeves**.

The distributors, agents, retailers and **knitters** who support all my books and yarns, and make all my projects possible.

Editorial Director **Jane O'Shea**
Creative Director **Mary Evans**
Project Editor **Lisa Pendreigh**
Editorial Assistant **Sarah Jones**
Photographer **Ulla Nyeman**
Stylist **Julie Mansfield**
Illustrator **Kate Simunek**
Pattern Illustrator **Bridget Bodoano**
Production Director **Vincent Smith**
Production Controller **Ruth Deary**

First published in 2008 by
Quadrille Publishing Limited
Alhambra House
27–31 Charing Cross Road
London WC2H 0LS
www.quadrille.co.uk

Text and project designs © 2008 Debbie Bliss
Photography, design and layout © 2008
Quadrille Publishing Limited

British Library Cataloguing-in-Publication Data
A catalogue record for this book is available from the British Library.

ISBN: 978 184400 612 0

Printed in China